"HOW are You DOING That?"

A Step-by-step Guide to
Effective Bible Clubs in
America's Public Schools

ROBERT C. HEATH

How Are You Doing That?
ISBN: 0-88144-325-5
Copyright © 2008 Robert Heath
2608 W. Kenosha #342
Broken Arrow, OK 74012
Website: www.kfcusa.org.

Printed by
YORKSHIRE PUBLISHING GROUP
7707 East 111th, Suite 104
Tulsa, OK 74133
www.yorkshirepublishing.com

Endorsements

"I am convinced after reading this book that every Children's Pastor in America should be ministering in a Bible Club."

—Chris Elia, Station Manager, TBN, New York

"Wow! Bob has answered "The Call" and now equips you in this great "manual" as he helps us all obey the "Go ye" commission. There are 45 million students/souls waiting to hear the good news of Jesus Christ in America's public school buildings. God is using Bob's help in public schools while transforming the lives of countless children. Thanks to Bob's obedience, sacrifice and willingness to share his ministry, you too can make a difference in America's modern day Canaan Land."

—"Armadillo Jim" Schmidt,
President: Put On Your Armor Foundation,
Author: *Helping Public Schools...Bridging the Gap*

"I have heard it said that it takes 8 million gallons of fuel to launch a rocket. Bob Heath has provided the fuel and then some to launch a revolution of the love of God in the lives of our children, our families, our schools and our communities. This book gives you the instruction and the inspiration to make a difference in children's lives today! I believe Kids For Christ is looking through God's eyes of compassion and reaching out with His hands of mercy to love our children in this present day!"

—*Brad Larson, Lead Pastor,*
The Life at Scottsdale

"No one I know is more passionate about reaching kids for Christ than Bob Heath. This book will both inspire you and equip you on how to transform your children's schools into a harvest field. Thanks Bob for helping us all to realize that our schools are not God forsaken places just church forsaken."

—*Roger Nix, Senior Pastor*
Believers Church, Tulsa, OK

Robert Heath brings his readers along on the journey of establishing student Bible Clubs through Kids for Christ USA. In the process he has created a "how to" handbook for a successful school campus outreach overflowing with creative ideas. This book is a must read for anyone wanting to impact youth on our public school campuses in America.

Now more than anytime in the history of this great nation, our public schools are a mission field ripe for the harvest. The sharing of our faith in the public sector is legal in our nation and it is required in His Kingdom.

—Finn Laursen, Executive Director,
Christian Educators

Table of Contents

The Ticket to Heaven Prayer

Overview of Teaching Material: Monthly Themes

Program Plan

Teaching Outlines

Whipped Cream Fountain

Whipped Cream Slurp

Whipped Cream Slurp (Variation 2)

Jello Slurping

Jello Eating (Variation 1)

Jello Eating (Variation 2)

Bobbing for Ravioli

Dirty Diaper Eating Contest

Baby Food Slurp

Pickles Eating Contest

The Pickle Dog

Making Pickle Juice

Pickle Juice Drinking Contest

Pickle Juice Drinking Contest (Variation 2)

Jelly Filled Pickle

Pudding Face

Silly String Glasses

Acting Class

Acting Class Part 2

Frozen Waffle Tossing

CoCo Puff Relay

CoCo Puff Relay (Variation 2)

Making Sandwiches

Gargle a Tune

Ice Cream Surprise

Hula Hoop Relay

Hula Hoop Transfer

Traditional Hula Hoop Contestant

Introduction

"Mom! Dad! Wake up!" These words boom out of your child's mouth as he races into your bedroom.

"Please get up!" Your son gently nudges your side and pushes into your arm. "You've got to get me to school early today!"

Your eyelids slowly open and your eyes start to focus. You're shocked with what you see first. Your son is already dressed for school and is even holding your car keys!

"It's Kids for Christ day," he says emphatically. "And I don't want to miss it!"

Does such a scene sound impossible? I've lived the normal reality with sleepy-headed children who refuse to get dressed for school. I've fought the endless morning battles just to get a child out of bed and ready for the day. I know how ridiculous this may sound to you, yet I also know after talking to hundreds of parents that a scene just like this one happens all across America as kids prepare to attend their weekly Bible Club meeting.

I've also heard a related scenario: kids begging parents to let them stay at school late in order to attend a weekly after-school Bible Club program.

Perhaps you too will hear stories just like this as you begin your own Bible Club. But before you print up your flyers and set up your weekly schedule, it's probably wise to start with a solid foundation that will prepare you for what you're going to encounter. I've written this book in order to help equip you with the knowledge, skills and insight needed to run an effective Bible Club in an American Public School.

I've been asked many questions since Kids for Christ USA, Inc. was formed. Without a doubt, the one I've been asked the most is: **"How are you doing that?"**

This most practical of all questions is usually followed closely with, "What about separation of church and state?" And we can't forget my personal favorite of all questions: "Wasn't the Bible banned from the public schools?"

In this book you'll find the astounding answers to each of these questions. If I had a dollar for every time I've been asked these questions, I could fund a ministry at least twice the size of this one!

My first attempt to answer these questions happened only six months after founding a Bible Club in our first school. I sat down and wrote a 21 page document that became known as the "Training Manual." Well, what you are about to read is that "Manual," repackaged for the fifth time in six years. The previous four versions were the nuts and bolts of this book. What you about to read explains how to launch a Bible club in an American public elementary school. This version also covers legal information that most people (Christian or not) don't know about....including me until December of 2005. Finally, this book discusses my philosophy of ministry within the schools and includes curriculum and loads of creative ideas for how to reach a new generation of Kids for Christ.

My personal journey began January of 2001. Since then, I have taught, learned, experienced, rejoiced and sacrificed much in order to bring this ministry to the children and families of this great nation. My team and I have worked hard to build a ministry that will annihilate the myth that "God isn't welcome in America's public schools."

I have said many times, "If there is one child in a school that has given his or her life to Jesus, then Jesus is in that school." **More than once Jesus said, "I will never leave you or forsake you."** You may have noticed that **He didn't say:** "I will never leave you or forsake you unless you go into a public school in America. That's it, that's where I draw the line." It makes the whole "Godless school system" concept seems a bit ridiculous when you hear it like that, doesn't it?

What is really amazing is that in my research I have uncovered evidence that proves that much of our belief regarding the Bible and prayer in the public school system is based on hearsay and media spin. Are you shocked? Let me explain the common foundation. For over forty years, we have talked about, preached about and complained about the Bible and prayer being removed from America's Public schools. BUT THAT DIDN'T EVEN HAPPEN! (I will explain what I mean in a later chapter.)

The book you are about to read is meant to equip you with all of the tools and information you'll need to go out and launch a Before or After School Bible Club in any school in

America. My goal is to inspire you and eliminate the intimidation you might feel when preparing to launch an endeavor such as this one.

One of the goals of this ministry is to have a hand in planting or facilitating a thriving Kids for Christ, USA-style Bible Club meeting every week in every school in America. I pray that after you read this book, you will not just be ready to go out and launch a club, but that you will also feel well advised and fully equipped to go out and do it well. If you feel inspired and illuminated after reading this book, then I have done my job.

So now, without further hesitation, let's start to explore "How You Do That."

SECTION I:

"Why Would You Do That?"

"The Kingdom of Heaven is like yeast used by a woman making bread. Even though she used a large amount of flour, the yeast permeated every part of the dough."

—Matthew 13:33 (New Living Translation)

No other verse in the Bible better sums up the vision of Kids for Christ USA, Inc. than Matthew 13:33 does. We are reaching children that might otherwise have been un-reached with the gospel.

A friend of mine once said, "If you want to reach the un-churched in Tulsa, or in any city in America, you'll find them in the public elementary and junior high schools. Once they are older than that, you're dealing with the Christ rejecters." We not only minister to children in the schools, but we teach them to minister God's love to their friends and family members. Therefore, we are training them to be evangelists and are turning them into the yeast of the dough that is their public school.

President George W. Bush was interviewed immediately following his inauguration in January of 2001. In that interview, he was asked what was to be his first priority? I remember vividly his response because I felt somewhat connected to it. He stated that "reform of the public schools" was his first priority. I am well aware that his intent was reform of the public school system, but I believe that God's intent is reform through revival in our public schools.

I was born in 1963. That is the year when mandatory Bible reading and mandatory prayer were removed from America's public schools and cut out of many children's daily lives. I remember vividly (as you may also) growing up and feeling scared that I would be suspended if I even admitted being a Christian, let alone shared my faith with a friend. I was saved when I was five years old, but there was no way I was going to give a friend a ticket to heaven. I was in the 9th grade before I even tried to witness to an unsaved friend, and that was at a youth retreat. Perhaps you can relate with me. I was so far from being "yeast" that whenever I would hear the verse quoted about being lukewarm, I would get real nervous because I didn't want to be spewed out of God's mouth.

It seems odd to go from that spiritually intimidated boy to a man who now runs a ministry that is determined to see that every child in the United States has the opportunity to partici-pate in a Bible club at his or her school.

Why would I, or any logical man take on an endeavor such as Kids for Christ, let alone one as big as Kids for Christ USA?

I wish my answer was as spiritually deep as Malachi 4:5: *"Look, I am sending you the prophet Elijah before the great and dreadful day of the Lord arrives. His preaching will turn the hearts of the fathers to their children and the hearts of the children to their fathers..."* (New Living Translation). In honesty, you need to understand that I often appear "dull" when it comes to following God. I had a Pastor who used to tell me that I was as "transparent as glass." I still am. Please understand that I am not talking about myself in an effort to be exalted as someone special. Quite the contrary; it's to show you that **if I can do this, ANYONE CAN.**

My story begins in the late 1990's. That's when I was thrust into children's ministry ... Actually, it was more like dragged ... kicking and screaming ... into children's ministry. I was attending a church back then that had a very obvious need for a children's ministry, but apparently only three (maybe five) of us knew it.

After a failed attempt to keep my oldest son, Brayden, in the main sanctuary for church, I was standing in the church foyer holding a crying four-year-old while God was busy talking to my heart. I argued with God, telling Him all the reasons why I was not a Kids' minister, which was of course an exercise in futility. I told him that a Children's Pastor was needed in that church. After all, "Pastor" was what I heard in my heart. So I brokered a deal with God (well, so I thought). I told Him what the Senior Pastor's response had to be if I were going to volunteer. Little did I fully understand that God already had a Plan and I was to be a part of it. So each of the parameters I laid out for God in "my deal" were met. Now I just had to follow through and do what I promised Him I would do.

So I was launched into the children's ministry as a Children's Pastor.

During the time I spent working with the children of that particular church, I began to conduct festival-style ministry within the community. As a result, I was invited to speak at a Bible Club in a local public school. It turned out to be a life changing experience. I ministered to 100 children in a standard-sized classroom and saw 12 children give their lives to Jesus that day. I remember driving away and praying, "Father, I could really see that as an effective tool to reach the lost and un-churched." Of course, once again I thought I was so wise, like I was actually telling God something that He didn't already know!

It wasn't long afterwards that God led me to step down and prepare for the next phase of ministry. I obeyed, but I also believed that God was finally going to show my wife, Shelly, and I where we were to go and plant a church. After all, He had now given me all these wonderful unconventional ideas for evangelism, so it must be time.

WRONG!

"Leadership is an act of service."

I spent the next two years learning that leadership is an act of service. The first and hardest part of this servant hood lesson started with my will. By then, I was assisting another ministry within the youth department. This caused me to be stretched so much that I truly considered having my name legally changed to "Gumby." But I was also blessed during this time with the privilege of serving with a Pastor who helped me "Take the lids off of my dreams." During my two years of learning to lead as a servant, God used this brilliant 25-year-old Pastor as a vehicle to instill within me many Biblical and natural truths. One of which was that "No one cares how much you know until they know how much you care." In children's ministry, I have seen that concept to be true. Let me restate that. I have *especially* seen this to be true when it comes to children's ministry.

A mother whose child attended my son's school found out that I had been a "Kid's Minister." She must have approached me at least three or four times during that two-year time period and asked me to launch a Bible Club at her school. (Of course, I didn't want to do it. So those three or four times *felt* like two or three dozen times.) I always replied to her the same way: "No! You have the wrong guy!" After all, I was going to Pastor a church one day. I was *not* going to oversee some cute Bible Club! As you can already tell, my plans and God's Plan tend to be light years apart. And as usual, I was slow to figure out where God was leading me in my life. (I'd like to think that I'm getting a bit more attentive to His leading. But my name is still

Bob Heath. And, well, He hasn't renamed me like he did Abraham and Moses.)

It was October of 2000 when God's plan finally collided with my ability to resist Him. This happened on "Dad's Day" in my son, Boston's class. I was sitting there minding my own business, sipping Kool-Aid and munching on cookies. Suddenly, a man I affectionately call "A Loose Cannon" walked into the room. As I looked up, I saw this guy handing gospel tracts to the dads in the room. He boldly asked them, "If you died today, do they know where you'll go?"

I remember thinking, "God, guys like him are why the schools think that we Christians are trouble makers." I'm sure I even rolled my eyes. But this guy didn't miss a single man, so he finally came and stood in front of me. I instantly became Balem's donkey.

He asked me, "Do you know where you'll go if you died?" I quickly responded. "Yes, I do know. I would go straight to heaven." The next moment is when the donkey part happened. It was literally as if I were not there, as if someone else had hijacked my voice. I heard myself ask him, "If I sponsored a Bible Club in this school, would you help me?"

"What's a Bible Club," he asked. I explained to him that it would be a full blown children's church service held right there in the school before classes started. OF COURSE HE ANSWERED, "YES!" And then I came to my senses. I quickly realized what had just happened: GOD HAD DONE IT AGAIN!

Oh, I failed to mention that the dad I was talking to before the Loose Cannon approached me was the husband of the lady who had been asking me for over two years to start Kids for Christ in that school. So it all boiled down to timing and to God using those around me to accomplish His Will. I still think it's pretty funny how it all came about.

Everything started moving fast, too. The next day, I sat in a meeting with the principal of the school and officially began to launch Kids for Christ in that school. The next step was to call a few people and figure out what I had gotten myself into. Yet God stood beside me all the way, confirming that I was walking in His will. In the same day, two different people said the exact same phrase to me. "The public schools are the greatest mission field in America." (I think some people in Tulsa, OK thought that was my own statement; now the truth is out about when I first heard it.) I also talked to at least four parents in my community. These parents were sponsoring Bible Clubs in their children's schools, but they were burned out, frustrated, and in one case in over their heads. I knew I had to prepare myself if I was going to avoid becoming another burned out parent.

While all of these preliminary details were falling into place, God dropped another crazy idea into my heart. I felt led to build an organization that would become the ultimate resource for students and parents wishing to sponsor Bible Clubs in America's public schools. When I shared this idea with those two people who had made the comment that the schools were a mission field, they both confirmed that the idea was probably a "God idea." Please keep in mind that I hadn't even held my first Club meeting yet, and suddenly I am thinking about starting a national movement. By the time we launched that first Club, I was already helping other parents plan their own Bible Clubs that were to start in the fall.

So it was January of 2001 when my Bible Club was kicked off at my son's school. I had no idea how many children to expect, but I would have been thrilled if 30-45 children came. To my complete surprise, we had 77 children that first day. My Teacher Sponsor pulled me aside at the end of the meeting and informed me that we had exceeded fire code for that room. (We were in the Library.) So the club would be moved to the Art Room the next week. Meeting number two brought 89 students and 12 altar responses. We continued to grow rapidly and soon outgrew the Art Room. This all happened within five weeks. On the sixth week, we cracked 100 and continued to grow up to 160 by March.

"So Bob, Why Would You Do This?"

I can tell you with absolute certainty that I was hooked for life after the first week. Sometime after that, in the first four weeks of the program at my son's school, a first grade girl who's family previously did not attend church responded to the altar call at the end of the meeting. She went home and told her mom about it and guess who was there the next Wednesday? You guessed it: Mom. I dare you to guess who gave their life to Jesus at the end of the meeting that day? Yes. You're right again. Mom. That weekend Mom, Dad, Daughter and Baby Brother all went to church. That's where Dad gave his life to Christ. This girl is now in the 7th grade and has lead no less than three of her peers to Jesus. She has one of the most tender hearts toward the hurting and lost I have ever encountered. We have at least two other documented stories like this one.

Perhaps reaching the un-churched isn't what encourages you to "Do This." Maybe for you it's seeing believers act on what they've been taught that moves you. We have stories like this, as well.

One morning after the Club meeting was over at my son's school, I was approached by a chubby African American 3rd grade girl.

"Mr. Bob, Mr. Bob," she said with enthusiasm. The room was still rather loud, so I knelt down to listen to her.

"Mr. Bob, My Daddy was doing bad things."

My mind took those words and began to run with them. I covered my mouth with my hand. "What kind of bad things was your Daddy doing?"

"Bad things! Mr. Bob he was doing them right in front of me."

Now I must admit that I was getting nervous. My idea of "bad things" was that maybe Daddy was doing something sexually inappropriate. This was also based on the emotion expressed by this little girl as she talked. In fact, I was thinking I was going to have to go talk to the school counselor and even call the Department of Human Services.

I cautiously queried her, "What kind of bad things was Daddy doing?"

"I was watching TV and he came into the room and started getting drunk."

WOW!!! That was the "bad things" she was talking about. Now please don't misunderstand me. I am not condoning Daddy getting drunk in front of his daughter, but I was so glad I had my mouth covered, because I almost laughed out loud (but I didn't, though). And I know that the smile I was covering would have seemed inappropriate, too.

Now I felt much more confident. I asked her, "What did you do?"

"Mr. Bob, I did exactly what you told me to do."

Naturally, I was a little confused and had to think about what I've said. I asked her, "And what was that?"

"I pointed my finger at him and I said, 'IN JESUS' NAME, YOU STOP IT!'"

Relieved, I was at this point about to fall over laughing. I managed to keep my cool as I asked her, "What did your Daddy do?"

She exclaimed, "Why he put down his beer and he went to work!"

Now to be really honest, I don't remember teaching any of this in any Club. I do, however, believe that every Christian should be confident in the authority the Bible says is ours through the death, burial and resurrection of our savior Jesus Christ. That young lady will not likely ever forget that faith-building experience. It fires me up to think that she may live her life being bold like that in the face of our adversary. If you're in to "building children of faith," then a story like this should be enough to motivate you to "Do This."

In fact, there are many great testimonies that answer the question, "Why Would You Do It?" But I really believe that not enough emphasis is placed on what is said in Matthew 6:33. *"...He will give you all you need from day to day __IF YOU LIVE FOR HIM AND MAKE THE KINGDOM OF GOD YOUR PRIMARY CONCERN.__* (New Living Translation— italics, capitalization and underlining added for emphasis).

I am not a big fan of denominations, denominationalism or doctrinal arguments. I don't think Jesus is, either. What really moves me is seeing the Love of God, empowering people, reaching the lost and un-churched, building and bringing the "Body of Christ" to a focus place of fellowship. I also love the idea of raising the next generation of leaders.

We teach the children a simple prayer they can use to lead their friends and family members to Jesus. God gave this prayer to a former team member and it has become a cornerstone to this ministry. The basic idea is the old adage of "if you give a man a fish, you feed him for a day, but if you teach him to fish, you feed him for a lifetime." Part of this concept is that if a child learns to lead their peers to Jesus, then they take a huge step toward establishing a relationship with God that is their own, instead of living on their parents' faith. I am often asked if I really think the Ticket to Heaven Prayer is an effective tool? "After all, they are just children" is often the comment. The following e-mail was received from an ecstatic mom. Please note that these are her exact words:

> I just wanted to share with you that our daughter, who is quite and shy, shared the ticket to heaven prayer with her 2nd grade class on October 3, 2005 at her school. She asked the class "who would like to have Jesus in their heart" and all 18 raised their hands and she said "just say this prayer with me," which was the ticket to heaven prayer. As her parents, we wanted to celebrate her courage and invited all the kids to Chuck E. Cheese on Friday, October 14 so that we can have an opportunity to find out if they have questions.
>
> One of the great stories this week as we received our responses was from the dad of a little girl in the class who said "I am so glad my daughter met your daughter, now she has Jesus in her heart." Awesome!

We have RSVP's from 11 of the 18 children and their families who are coming this evening to Chuck E Cheese's and we are excited about the opportunity to share more.

Thank you for your organization Kids For Christ; my daughter and I attend on Tuesday afternoons at our school.

Blessings,
A Proud Mommy

This mom called me after the party and told me what happened. All eleven children who came to the party at Chuck E. Cheese with their families "validated" their earlier commitment. I know some readers may be wondering if this little girl violated any laws. The short answer is: NO. She shared the ticket to heaven prayer with her friends during her free time when the school day was over. She did not do this during class time or "instructional time." The law will back up a child who shares at the "right time." Passing out tracts and talking about Jesus during FREE time is allowed under Federal law. (I have much to say about the legal rights of the students and their parents in the next section.)

Operation What?

Almost every year we do a group project using the Ticket to Heaven Prayer. Our most successful project is Operation Big Bird. We spend a month getting the children ready for thanksgiving dinner. We encourage them to volunteer to pray for their family's Thanksgiving dinner. They lead their entire family in the "Ticket to Heaven Prayer" and add, "...Father, please bless the food in Jesus' name. Amen." This event has been wildly successful throughout the years. One year over 1,100 people prayed with 500+ children at the Thanksgiving table. The best we could estimate, it appears that there could have been over 400 decisions that year.

This gave me an idea for Halloween. We called it "Operation Treat or Treat." We don't encourage children to go trick or treating, yet we realize they are going to go, so we instead encourage the kids to go to the door and say, "Treat or Treat." This was an idea that was going to take a very courageous child to pull off. In honesty, the project has not been nearly as successful as Operation Big Bird. Or has it? One year after we did this project, a dad shared his story with me in his own words:

> When I first heard of the idea, I must say I wasn't sure about it. My son Drew, 11 years old at the time, came home the week before Halloween and excitedly told me his plans for the night of trick or treat. He told me that in his weekly Kids for Christ Bible study at his elementary school, he was taught how to evangelize the Gospel of Christ to strangers in a simple, effective manner. He was taught the scriptural principles of salvation through Christ Jesus, and was also taught a simple

prayer to lead a person to Christ. If he would have stopped there, I would have had no hesitations. However, Drew proceeded to tell me that he was encouraged to implement this plan at EVERY DOOR he knocked on as he went trick or treating! As I hid my reluctance of the idea, I reached deep for an enthusiastic "hey, that sounds great; I can't wait to see how it goes!" In the back of mind, I was wrongly concerned for a couple of different reasons.

One reason was that at the time, Drew had a severe speech impediment. It was so bad at this period in his life that many attempts at speaking resulted only in strange facial contortions followed by a failed exasperated attempt at communication, which usually ended in frustration by both parties. I just did not know how well an evangelistic message by an 11-year-old who could barely speak would be received. Another reason for concern was that I erroneously worried that Drew would be rejected and even perhaps made fun of. After all, this was his first year to trick or treat without the constant presence of an adult, and two of his friends would be with him. What would they think of this idea?

I would love to exaggerate and embellish a spectacular ending to this story that included a supernatural healing of his speech, universal acceptance of Drew and his message by every door that was knocked on, and dozens of people led to Christ. But God does not need His works exaggerated or embellished. Although none of these things happened, what actually did happen blessed me even more. Drew happily reported at the end of the night, that "most people were nice and patient, some closed the door on me, and nobody let me pray with them." At first glance this courageous effort by an 11-year-old boy trick or treating with two other 11-year-old friends may appear to be disappointing or uneventful at best. But the story goes further.

You see, months before, Drew prayed in faith ONCE for his healing based on the Word of God. He then THANKED God for his healing every night since, patiently awaiting the manifestation. You see, Drew KNEW he was healed ALREADY, despite his unchanged circumstances and symptoms, because God said in His Word that he was healed. So Drew boldly went forth, without hesitation or embarrassment, with this evangelism. To Drew, his speech was whole, because God said it was; not because he FELT like it was.

Furthermore, after getting details about the night of getting candy and sharing Christ, I learned that most assuredly many seeds were sown in the hearts of many from this 11-year-old child of God. Drew was used by God in the EXACT manner in which God desired that night. In addition, Drew proved to himself that indeed he CAN do all things through Christ who strengthens him (one of his favorite verses). Sharing the Gospel is an anointed event, and Drew learned that he could do it, and do it with courage and boldness derived from God. At an early age, he learned a lesson that many of us do not get until much later in life, if at all.

So at the end of the day, we see how God can miraculously work in the lives of children (and the adults around them) in the absence of a spectacular event. Kids for Christ nurtured Drew's spirit, and I am certain will continue to do so. As a side note, Drew received his manifestation of whole speech 8 months later. Although still speaking with a mild bit of difficulty, his speech is 85-90% of what it will eventually be; which is perfect. And as a true child of faith, he will tell you that he was more excited about his healing when it actually occurred—the night heprayed, which was 18 months before the manifestation.

—Written by a very proud Dad

I love that story for so many reasons, both theological and parental ones. I love that Drew's Dad didn't discourage him in any way. He let his son take a spiritual risk, a step of faith toward developing a real relationship with God for himself. In my ever so humble opinion, when we as parents shelter our children spiritually, we potentially hinder their ability to learn how to stand on their own faith. The same is true naturally speaking; as parents, we need to give our children tools to grow and then take a really bold step: Let them grow. Drew's dad did that. I personally know Drew and I can tell you that he is a young man with a heart after God.

Since we minister to so many un-churched children, I am of the belief that there are certain "building blocks" that it is imperative we mold into the children's character. The one I feel most strongly about is worship. We are all worshippers, but if a child learns to worship God, then the likelihood of a strong relationship with God is increased. After all, we were created to worship God. If a child doesn't learn to worship God then he or she will eventually worship *something*. Our meetings typically last for only 30 minutes, so we don't have a lot of time to spend on worship. Quality over quantity is the aim. There is nothing like seeing a group of kids in a public school worshiping God in unity. This is a concept kids seem to understand more than adults do. When they come together in a Bible Club, they don't come together as a group of Baptists, Methodists, Lutherans, Charismatic, (Insert your denomination here) heathen. They just dive in and worship God with all of their hearts.

I remember a few years ago in a particular elementary school asking the kids if there were any prayer requests. I went to the back of the room to pray with the three kids who had raised their hands. While I was in the back praying, my worship leader was leading the kids in the song, "I Could Sing of Your Love Forever." I was conscious of the song and semi-listening as I prayed with the kids. I had to do this because I needed to be back in the front of the room when the worship leader finished the song. When I finished praying, I stood up, turned around, and to my utter shock I saw all 77 kids in that room worshiping God with their eyes closed and their hands up. I quietly slipped to the front and whispered in my leader's ear, "Did you tell them to close their eyes and lift their hands?" She shook her head "No." I was astounded; I had never seen that kind of pure-hearted unity even in an adult service! Whatever your denominational affiliation may be, you couldn't deny God's presence there that day. That unity in worship was the beginning of something even more amazing. During the following semester, the kids in that Club were so filled with a desire to please God that they led over 400 people to Jesus using the Ticket to Heaven Prayer. Many were their classmates, neighbors, family members and even a teacher. It was amazing!

Something similar happened during worship in a Junior High Kids for Christ Club. Eighty-eight seventh graders shocked the bejeebers out of me one morning. (And I didn't even know

I had bejeebers.) I can honestly say that I was totally oblivious to what was going on at first. We met in one of the band rooms of that school and as the kids came into the room, many of them did just as kids will do: they dropped their backpacks down on the floor as they walked through the door. So, I was behind them moving backpacks so that more kids could get into the room. I knew it was about time for me to head toward the front of the room to teach the kids. When I turned around, I became aware that something special was happening. I saw all the kids worshipping in their own way. I SAID ALL OF THE KIDS! It was somewhat overwhelming. Even the two guys in the back of the room who usually talked all the time were singing and swaying back and forth as they worshiped God. As I began to approach the front of the room, I began to feel the uncontrollable urge to cry. I stopped, waited and watched. It was beautiful. There was a boy from a Charismatic background in the far corner dancing as he worshipped. There were three girls in the front row crying as they sang. There wasn't anyone holding back or trying to be cool (like 7th graders typically do). I finally reached the front of the room, ready to preach, but unwilling to interrupt what God was doing that morning. I took the microphone and told the kids, "I can teach you, in fact I have part two of the series I started last week ready to share, but if you guys want to continue to give God your best in worship, then I don't have to teach. It's your call." In unison across the room, they all said, "We want to worship!" I walked to the back of the room where no one could see me, dropped to my knees and wept.

That must be what the "Upper Room" felt like on the day of Pentecost. (All 120 people in one accord.)

These are just a few of the many amazing experiences that I can recall since January 2001. There are so many more experiences that I've had or heard about. When I recall these stories, I can't help but answer the question with a responding, **"Why wouldn't I do this?"** Why should you do this? Because it is one of the most rewarding experiences a believer can ever have.

Section II:

"How Are You Doing That?"

As I stated in the previous section, the most commonly asked questions about Kids for Christ are:

1. "How are you doing that?"
2. "What about separation of church and state?"
3. "Is it legal?"

I also mentioned United States citizenship and paralleled it with understanding the concept of "who and what the Bible says we are in Christ." I stated that the answer to "how we do what we do" is best answered after you understand your rights as a citizen of both the Kingdom of God and the United States. What I didn't say was something that I didn't even realize at first. Christians and United States citizens in general usually do not understand their legal rights. I think this is because the "church" and the "state" have something else in common: a belief that we should leave the truths of the Bible to the

Preachers and the facts in the Constitution to the lawmakers. After all, we are encouraged to believe that the common man can't understand the Bible of the Constitution, anyway. Consequently, we have made ourselves slaves to our own ignorance. I feel a little like the apostle Paul must have felt when he said, "I would not have you ignorant..." So, let me explain a few legal issues before I actually tell you how we run a Bible club. My goal is to instill in you the confidence you'll need to launch and sustain an effective Bible Club in any American public school.

As you can imagine, I did do a significant amount of research when I first began my journey. I needed to understand where I stood legally to make sure I was functioning within the law. During the course of my research period, I hopped online and used the Internet to learn about the exact date when prayer was removed from America's schools. I knew in my mind that it was either 1962 or 1963. So I pulled up Google and typed in the phrase, "Bible and Prayer removed from America's public schools." I was shocked by the search results. One of the first ones bore this title: "Myth 8: O'Hair removed God / Bible / Prayer from schools." Naturally, I was extremely intrigued by this, so I clicked on the link and read the article. I read something that I had never read before. The article explained how Madelyn Murray O' Hair and a Philadelphia man named Ed Schempp challenged mandatory prayer and Bible reading. The result was not as I have heard all my life: **Only Mandatory Bible Reading and Prayer were removed from the public schools, BUT VOLUNTARY BIBLE READING AND**

VOLUNTARY PRAYER WERE NEVER REMOVED FROM OUR SCHOOLS!

Let me say that again: **God, the Bible, and Prayer were NEVER removed from America's Public Schools.**

Since this was the first time I had ever realized that only MANDATORY prayer and Bible reading had been removed, I continued to visit more web sites. (After all, this was fascinating; it was fully illuminating information that I now needed to verify.) I noticed that I had been reading from an atheist site, so I quickly clicked off and clicked another link. This time I pulled up an online brochure on the "Americans United for The Separation of Church and State" web site. This brochure stated that **"nothing in the 1962 or 1963 rulings makes it unlawful for public school students to pray or read the Bible (or any other religious book) on a voluntary basis during their free time."** Let me continue to quote from this brochure:

> Judge Tom Clark said of the 1963 Abington decision, 'The place of religion in our society is an exalted one, achieved through a long tradition of reliance on the home, the church, and the inviolable citadel of the individual heart and mind. We have come to recognize through bitter experience that it is not within the power of government to invade that citadel, whether its purpose or effect be to aid or oppose, to advance or retard. In the relationship between man and religion, the State is firmly committed to a position of neutrality.' He further said, 'It might well be said that one's education is not complete without a study of

comparative religion or the history of religion and its relationship to the advancement of civilization. It certainly
may be said that the Bible is worthy of study for its literary
and historic qualities. Nothing we have said here indicates
that such study of the Bible or of religion, when presented
objectively as part of a secular program of education, may
not be affected consistently with the first amendment.

Let me recap what I found on the Americans United for the
Separation of Church and State web site:

**Voluntary prayer and Bible reading *were never
removed* from the public school system.** Only MANDA-
TORY prayer and MANDATORY Bible reading were removed.
These facts have been largely distorted since that 1963 ruling.
My research did not allow me to pinpoint the source that started
this distortion of the truth. However, it's feasible that people
who were "in the know" said nothing while the ruling was
misinterpreted. This may have caused the misconception to
begin. According to a couple of atheist sites I visited and the
Americans United for the Separation of Church and State site, it
is a myth that Madelyn Murray O'Hair single-handedly removed
God, Prayer, and the Bible from America's public school. In
contrast to my previous statement, I did uncover an interesting
fact that only makes it harder to determine how this distortion
of the truth began. I was reviewing a law site when I ran across
an article written by her son, William Murray. He described his
mother as being pure evil in that article. He also stated that she
often bragged about being the one responsible for single-handedly removing prayer and the Bible from America's public

schools. I grew up hearing ministers and even Christian musicians describing her the same way and also citing her as being responsible for removing prayer and the Bible from school. That's why I grew up believing I was not allowed to even mention the name of Jesus at school. This distortion of the truth runs so deep in our society that almost everyone, both Christians and non-Christians, believes it to be true. One thing is for sure: what is commonly believed is only A DISTORTION OF THE ACTUAL RULING. **Annihilating that distortion and wiping its deception from our society is a personal goal of mine.**

"...The Bible is worthy of study for its literary and historic qualities."—Judge Tom Clark. This statement paves the way for a Bible curriculum to be taught in the schools. Doing this is fully legal PROVIDED it is used only for historic and literary instruction. But keeping up with the spirit of the law means teaching from the Koran, Torah, Book of Mormon, etc. This is not something that many of us Christians want to hear. My feeling is that God's word will always prevail as truth, even if texts from all these religions were taught. This leads me to the next point:

"...The State is firmly committed to a position of neutrality." –Judge Tom Clark. This is a really interesting comment. I believe it is the "line in the sand" with regard to the debate over "separation of church and state." I'm sure you've heard of the concept of separation of church and state? (That is, I'm sure you have if you live in the U.S. and you breathe air.) Liberals who wish to keep God or the mere mention of God out of Government affairs keep the separation issue in front of us. I believe their purpose is intimidation. If you can intimidate people, then they are unlikely to act on their rights. Guess what? This practice works. That is why the distortion of the Bible and prayer being removed from the schools has been so effective. Well, according to what Judge Clark said, "The State is firmly committed to a position of neutrality." NEUTRALITY! As Justice O'Connor said, "If a State refused to let religious groups use facilities open to others, then it would demonstrate not neutrality but hostility toward religion." THAT'S IT! THAT'S THE LINE IN THE SAND! Does the action of the State demonstrate neutrality to all religions or hostility toward one religion?

We as Christians don't always agree about everything, but we must all remember that proper decisions with regard to Church and State means there cannot be hostility toward <u>any</u> specific religion. Not ours, not anyone else's. Likewise, this does not give the school the right to exclude all religious organizations, either. To do so could be interpreted as hostility toward religion. If we know the Power of God and we know His love, then we know that "it's not His will that any should perish but that all should have eternal life." We know that Jesus said, *"I am the way the truth and the life, no man comes to the Father but by me."* If that is understood, then when we stand in the face of persecution (hostility toward Christianity), then we can press on with confidence by the power of God. Just understand that part of the price you must pay to use a school (or any public facility) is that you may have to be in the same building preaching about Jesus while someone else is preaching about Buddha. That really shouldn't be an issue, if you truly believe in God's power.

The above quoted excerpts came from documents published by the Americans United for the Separation of Church and State. This information was also cited from a thorough briefing that the American Center of Law and Justice (which is more from a Christian perspective) and from Christian Educators Association International. All this information is available on the Internet as well. You will find the web addresses for these organizations listed in the bibliography. I advise you to study about this topic for yourself. There is a far more information posted on their web sites than I intend to share here. My opinion is that this is fascinating information and it is completely worth your time to review it. In fact, I hope you'll be like the Apostle Paul said of the Bereans in Acts 17. He said, *"These were more fair-minded (Or open minded) than those in Thessalonica, in that they received the word with all readiness, and searched the Scriptures daily to find out whether these things were so."* Well, this information may not come from the Scriptures, but if you study this topic for yourself, you will see that what I am saying is accurate and you will also build your faith as you add spiritual confidence.

Now, you're finally ready to hear "How We Do What We Do"

The Supreme Court has addressed the right of students to express their opinions on their public school campuses. Specifically, the Court has held that students and teachers do not "shed their constitutional rights ... at the schoolhouse gate." As a result, several years ago The Equal Access Act was passed. It was challenged and held up by the Supreme Court in the "Mergens Bible clubs case." They ruled that public secondary schools that receive federal funds and allow non-curriculum related clubs to meet on campus must also allow Bible clubs ("Bible clubs" also includes prayer groups) to meet on campus during non-instructional time. It is important to note that the 8th Circuit Court in the Mergens case held that students have a First Amendment right and an Equal Access Act right to hold a student-initiated Bible club meeting on campus. In layman's terms, High School students have the right to sponsor Bible Clubs during non-instructional time. The way that our educational system is set up, almost all public schools receive Federal funds. This means that if the school has clubs that are allowed to meet on campus that are not a part of a class that is being taught, or are not directly related to a school class, then the school must allow your Bible Club the same privilege. In other words, the school must give the Bible club or prayer group official recognition on campus. **If the school allows service type clubs such as Boy Scouts, Cub Scouts, Girl Scouts, Interact, Zonta, 4-H, or chess clubs, it must allow Bible Clubs.**

Perhaps you are thinking, "Well, that's great, but what about elementary schools?" My logical analysis of the law has always been, "If that is a first amendment right for a high school student who happens to be a minor, then the same right must be available to elementary students, especially those attending a Bible Club with the approval of their parent or guardian." Recently, I validated my logical analysis when I ran across a document posted on the Christian Educators Association International web site:

Even though the Equal Access Act does not apply to elementary schools, the First Amendment to the United States Constitution does. Therefore, if other student clubs are allowed on campus, then a Bible club would also be allowed.

That's pretty clear!

Earlier I stated that neutrality toward religion and instead of hostility is a key line in the sand. I went on and explained that if we as Christians are allowed to have a Bible Club, then Muslims, Hindus, or any other practice or religion can also have a club. That falls under the guidelines of Equal Access. Neutrality would apply even in the event that a school has not allowed any non-curriculum clubs to meet; the Tinker rule would still require that students be allowed to associate with other students in Bible Clubs. A few years ago, a school district in the Tulsa area refused to allow a parent I was working with to launch a club. They stated that since there were no clubs on campus (including Scouts; they met off campus), we couldn't meet there, either. At the time I had not learned about what is legally acceptable yet. Because of my ignorance back then, I agreed with what the school district said when my parent sponsor told me about it. I literally backed away. Now that I better understand the "Neutrality and Hostility issue," I would have advised that parent differently. The good news is that the parent was persistent and she just kept refining her approach and going back to the school district until she got approval. Sometimes that's what it takes. Occasionally, legal action is needed, but that is the exception, not the rule. PLEASE remember that you are a Christian and anything you do reflects on your Christian witness. So please remember that taking legal action is an absolute LAST RESORT.

Once the Bible Club is officially recognized, it must be allowed to advertise on campus. The Club has the right to use the public address system, the school bulletin boards, the school newspaper, and to even participate during club fairs. Thus, the students can use any form of media available to the other clubs to get the message out to the rest of the school.

Fliers distributed by students to their peers is an effective means of promoting the Club. Some schools have tried to prohibit this action because they are concerned that someone might complain when a child comes home with a flyer about a Christian club. Some school districts state that the Christian Club can use the same means of distribution as every other club in the school: A rack on the wall in or near the school office. This appears to be an act of equality, except that the Parent Teacher Association (PTA) is exempt from distributing its literature in the same manner. Since they are a "service organization," they are allowed to distribute their materials by hand to students and their families. If you look up the definition of a "Club," you find definitions such as, "A group of people organized for a common purpose, especially a group that meets regularly." Does that sound like the PTA to you? It sure does to me.

Students' First Amendment rights include the right to distribute Gospel tracts during non-instructional time, the right to wear shirts with overtly Christian messages and symbols, and the right to pray and discuss matters of religion with others. Further, schools may not prevent students from bringing their Bibles to school. In fact, school officials must allow students to read their Bibles during free time, even if that free time occurs during class.

As a matter of fact, it is a constitutional axiom that the distribution of free religious literature, such as tracts, is a form of expression protected by the First Amendment. This information comes from the ACLJ, citing Lovell v. City of Griffin, 303 U.S. 444 (1938); Widmar, 454 U.S. 263, 269 (1981). Religious and political speech are protected by the First Amendment. According to the American Center for Law & Justice (ACLJ), "The United States Supreme Court's consistent jurisprudence, for over 50 years, recognizes the free distribution of literature as a form of expression protected by the United States Constitution." I am not an attorney, but simple common sense says that this should include flyers for a Bible Club, especially when they are distributed by students (even if a parent stands nearby holding a box of flyers, such as in the case of elementary students).

The Supreme Court did not limit the rights of Bible Clubs in any way. Bible Clubs must be treated like any other club in the school, with full rights and privileges. The Bible Clubs must be allowed to meet before or after school or during a club period, just like any other club. The clubs have a right not only to meet, but also to reach other students with the message that the Bible Clubs are meeting.

If other clubs are allowed to have school-wide assemblies to espouse their views, then the Bible Club must be allowed the same privilege. School officials are not allowed to discriminate against a student group because of its message. I know of a Junior High School Bible Club in Pennsylvania that was allowed to have an assembly. The Christian Club did a year end concert for the entire school. Hundreds of kids came. The band (which was made up of other students) played, and at the end a 14-year-old young man of God shared his testimony and gave an altar call. Many of his peers responded and gave their lives to Jesus.

Before we go into the specifics about being a Parent or Student Sponsor (and the other elements necessary for running a Club), I feel the need to further liberate you with regard to certain legal issues. (I will save the legal information specific to teachers for the Teacher Sponsor section.) This is all pertinent in building your confidence in regard to where you stand legally.

Another myth: Public school students can't share their faith on their campus.

Quoting the ACLJ again:

> Our educational system requires students to attend schools. This coercion gives students the legal right to be on campus. As Justice Fortas noted: 'In our system, state-operated schools may not be enclaves of totalitarianism. School officials do not possess absolute authority over their students. Students in school as well as out of school are 'persons' under our Constitution. They are possessed of fundamental rights which the State must respect, just as they themselves must respect their obligations to the State. In our system, students may not be regarded as closed-circuit recipients of only that which the State chooses to communicate. They may not be confined to the expression of those sentiments that are officially approved. In the absence of a specific showing of constitutionally valid reasons to regulate their speech, students are entitled to freedom of expression of their views.' As Judge Gewin, speaking for the Fifth Circuit, said, 'school officials cannot suppress expressions of feelings with which they do not wish to contend.'

Based on this ruling, as well as rulings from two different cases, the Court reinforced students' right to evangelize on campus. We see from these cases that students have the right to share the love of God with their friends; this right is fully protected under the United States Constitution. Students can express their First Amendment rights and enjoy the freedom of religion on campuses across the country. **<u>School officials do not have the right to control student speech just because their speech is religious in nature.</u>** Students have the right to pass out Christian papers and tracts to their peers on campus. As long as the students do not disrupt school discipline, school officials must allow them to be student evangelists. It was argued that to allow the students to meet on campus and to act as student evangelists would violate the Establishment Clause of the First Amendment. However, this argument was rejected by the Court in the *Mergens case.* Thus, *Mergens* is a great victory for Christian high school students in America. With the decision in *Mergens,* the Supreme Court has sent a clear message to the school systems of America. No longer will religious discrimination be tolerated under the guise of "separation of church and state."

In a tight little nutshell, my research brought these points to light for me and paved the way for Kids for Christ USA to do what we do:

- The Bible and Prayer were never outlawed from public schools.

- Teacher mandated prayer and Bible reading was outlawed ... voluntary student prayer and Bible reading were not. Student prayer and Bible reading is allowed during free time at school.

- Bible Clubs are permissible during non-instructional time at school, especially if other clubs are allowed to meet, and perhaps even if other clubs are not allowed to meet.

- Students can always share their faith with other students.

- Bible Clubs are allowed to advertise by any means that other clubs are allowed to use: NO EXCEPTIONS! (The same as the PTA or Scouts.)

Student or Parent Sponsors:

Now, I guess the next thing to discuss is "Your approach" when it comes time to talk to Mr. or Mrs. Principal.

In order for Kids for Christ USA, (KFCUSA) Child Evangelism Fellowship (CEF) or your best friend to help you with a program in an elementary, junior high or high school, a student or parent sponsor is needed. I remember the first day of Kids for Christ at my son's school. What I did was (and still is) both challenging and incredibly rewarding. I remember walking out of that school saying to God, "You know, Lord, that was incredible! I could do that for the rest of my life." Knowing that you had a hand in reaching lost souls in your child's school is a wonderful feeling. I have no words to describe the awesome blessing of this simple act of service. You are the frontline person in your child's school. Even if we (or some other group) assist you, you are still the liaison between the school and that group. The goal I had when I started Kids for Christ USA was to instill confidence in students and parent sponsors across the country. You are not alone! For starters, Jesus said, "I will never leave you or forsake you." He also referred to the Holy Spirit as the comforter: Whom he was sending. So you have God's promise to be there for you. You also have access to groups like KFCUSA and CEF who can be a resource for you to use in whatever capacity you need.

As you have just read, the laws regarding Bible Clubs are written with the junior high and high school students in mind. That is because those students and their families fought this battle that has already paved the way for us. The laws say that a club must be student sponsored and student initiated. However, at the elementary level, there is no legal precedent as yet, so most schools will allow a "parent sponsor" to assist a student sponsor to organize the program. The reason is simple: it's just common sense that most elementary age children lack the organizational skills needed to operate a program like this. I was warned by the ACLJ in the beginning of this ministry that if I did what I said I wanted to do, I would probably be involved in setting those legal precedents at the elementary level. I used to think that a precedent was needed at this age, but I no longer think that. What I mean is that since it has been declared that it is a First Amendment right for students, then I am not sure that it is a worthwhile fight to graft elementary schools into the Equal Access Act.

Now let's get to that approach I mentioned at the beginning of this section.

If you were a shy kid who never acted out in class and was never sent to the principal's office, then this trip can be a bit unnerving. In fact, take it from me: IT WILL BE unnerving. Just remember the Word says that you will have *"peace that passes all understanding."* In my case, I felt like my chair was really small and like I was actually looking into the eyes of The President. I tried to speak, but no sound would come out of my lips. Then, when something did come out of my mouth, I sounded like Porky the Pi, Pi, Pi, Hog. (Please don't make me explain the joke.)

Remember this (but *not* with a militant attitude, PLEASE): You are an American Citizen. As such, you own that building because your taxes helped to pay for it. You have the right to use it for a Bible Club both before and after school. In other words, that Principal can't tell you "No" unless he or she plans to turn down the same club requests presented by the Boy Scouts, Cub Scouts, Girl Scouts, Little League Baseball, and any other extra-curricular group. You know that won't happen, so "fear not."

Just for the record, if you do have a problem, then contact Kid's for Christ USA immediately. Our web site, e-mail address, and phone number is listed in the back of this book. You can also call CEF. For legal help, you can also call upon The Alliance defense fund or the ACLJ. Please don't hesitate to contact us if you have any problems; we will be happy to help guide you through the process. In fact, I recommend that you program our phone number into your cell phone speed dial before you walk into that office. (Well, you can if you wish to; I was partly joking right here. More than likely you won't need to call us.)

It seems silly to say this, but the first order of business, even before you go to see the principal, is actually preparation. The most successful groups I have had the pleasure of working with coordinated a group of moms before they ever visited the Principal. Talk about a confidence builder! The lead Mom knew before she ever visited the Principal that she had several other moms who were standing by her. They broke down a list of responsibilities among themselves. When they did get the go ahead from the school, they were ready. I advise you to go as prepared as possible, both naturally and spiritually. And remember, the most important confidence builder is caused by taking some time to be alone with God before you head off to the school.

One More Suggestion: Connect with Moms in Touch

Another great resource is "Moms in Touch" prayer groups. This National organization functions very similar to how KFCUSA functions. They break down from National all the way down to the school level. Talk about powerful; a group of moms who meet weekly for the sole purpose of praying and serving the school their child attends! As you prepare your Club, connect with the regional offices of Moms in Touch. If they have a group in your school, I recommend that you connect with them and even join them. Wherever KFCUSA goes, we have noticed that the Clubs that have student or parent sponsors who took the time to connect with the local Moms in Touch group ends up with a Bible Club that THRIVES!

Meeting with the Principal

I know we haven't talked about teacher observers yet, but I would try to have at least an idea about who you want to have as your teacher observer before you visit the Principal. When you go, some of the items you need to remember to request are:

- A room in which to hold your meetings.

- A day and time for your meetings. (We have found it best to allow the Principal to choose the day.) This can be before or after school.

- A start time, roughly 50-60 minutes before school begins or 10-15 minutes after it ends. (This time frame is especially important if you intend to serve snacks.)

- If you wish to offer snacks, be sure to discuss that with the Principal. I advise you to be "up front" with the Principal from the start. In fact, get permission for everything you can think of during your initial meeting. Go ahead and ask to sponsor "See You at the Pole" in September. Ask permission to give candy as prizes, reward incentives ... whatever you think of, ask to do it ... now. The schools are no place to operate with the mentality of "It's easier to ask forgiveness than permission." Even though I think there is a place for that, the schools are not that place. That mentality is just asking for trouble in this type of program. Never assume permission. Ask for it!

- Also, it's always a good idea to offer to fill out any appropriate forms or complete any other necessary documentation. That way, you show that you want to do things "right."

Other Matters

This is hard for many to understand because they think in terms of church meetings, but your meeting should not exceed 40 minutes. This time frame *includes* snack time. I know CEF sponsored meetings typically run 90 minutes. That is the amount of time that their curriculum is tailored to fit. I am convinced that 40 minutes is plenty of time, if you don't waste your time. Most of the groups I have been privileged to assist meet before school. So, consequently, it would simply not be feasible to get the kids to school 95-100 minutes before class time. (Most parents won't bring children to the school between 6:30 and 7:00 A.M.) Not only that, but you probably wouldn't want to get there at 6:00 A.M. to set up the room, either! (You'd most likely find it a bit tough to get any help with the program that early, too.) I personally believe that 40 minutes is as Goldie Locks said, "Just right." It is perfect for morning or afternoon attention spans.

The afternoon time slot (even though that's the specialty of CEF) is not recommended for your meetings. I realize that in some cases it might be the only option, so please don't be discouraged by my opinion if this is the only option you have. I know of several clubs that have worked better in the afternoon. (This proves that my theories are truly theories and not scientific facts.) It has been my experience that it's easier to teach the kids in the morning. They are more attentive before school starts. After school, there are more distractions that make keeping the children's attention very difficult and can create much frustration for you. It's just tough to get a "good crowd" in the afternoon.

Please remember that the amount of effort you put forth will radically affect the success of your club. We have watched this concept be proven to be true over and over again; schools with parent or student sponsors that get excited about the program and put forth a lot of effort see amazing rapid growth. (Both in numbers and in the spiritual lives of the kids.) One such school has been nothing short of astounding.

Next, you need to understand that **you will be the "host" of these weekly meetings and the kids are counting on you to be consistent.** You'll need to greet the children as they come in. One mom decided she wanted to take attendance and relayed the information to us, therefore allowing us to have a better sense of accountability with the children and their families. In some schools, permission slips are required, which makes the concept of taking attendance a priority so that you can be compliant. Most schools we've worked with don't require permission slips.

Another advantage to meeting in the morning is that the legal concept of implied consent makes permission slips unnecessary. Essentially implied consent assumes that a child (especially an elementary age child) would not be at the school an hour early without the consent of their parent or guardian. The same is true in the afternoon, but it's a little more difficult to make that assumption.

As the sponsor, it is important see to it that things are set up before meetings and cleaned up promptly afterwards. This means that the room you are blessed with can be used as a classroom again when you leave. Please don't operate with the attitude that the janitorial staff is there for the purpose of cleaning up after you. On the contrary, when it comes to cleaning up, "you need to make the room shine." (Sparkle, even.)

Beware of statements of apparent intimidation

When I started Kids for Christ at my son's school, the Principal said to me, "You know that if I allow you to meet, the same law that allows you to meet would allow other religions including Satanism to meet here as well?" That statement is true, and at the time, I told her I would bow out before that happened. Guess what? Even if I were to quit, those other religions are protected by the same laws ours is protected by. They can still be there, so why quit? After all, I serve the true and LIVING GOD!

I know of a school where the parent sponsor gave up when the Muslims said, "If you don't shut down that Christian Club, we will start one." This wasn't a Club I was involved in. Too many times, followers of Christ refuse to "call the bully out" with confidence that God, the Living God, the Father of our Lord Jesus Christ, is standing with us. Please understand that I'm not suggesting that we start religious wars. I am, however, saying we must seek God's wisdom, and then use that wisdom. That school has had no Bible Club (or Muslim Club) for two years now. THAT SHOULD NOT BE SO!

Several years ago, I received a call from a parent sponsor who was upset because it was looking like we might have a problem brewing. She proceeded to tell me that there was a Jewish teacher that was angry because we were having our Club meet in a classroom. She didn't think it was right that we continued the Club in that teacher's classroom past the time the teacher was required to begin working (also known as her "contract time").

"Bob I am afraid we might have to shut down," the parent told me almost in tears. I did something that shocks many of my Christian friends: I said to the mom, "Tell her that if she wants to start Kids for Judaism or Torah, I will provide the snacks." You see, I know that the Jews are God's chosen people, and those who bless the Jews will be blessed and those who don't, won't be blessed. Some people just can't believe I would say that because Jewish people don't profess Jesus as Messiah. I know, but they teach morality, and that would be an asset to the school's character program. Besides, I also know and understand that "you catch more bees with honey than vinegar." (My momma told me that one.) Well, it worked. The teacher was touched by the offer, and the situation was diffused.

The next logical question is: WHO DOES THE MINISTRY?

As a parent or student sponsor, the answer to this question is entirely up to you. One of the primary concerns many sponsors (whether they are students or parents) have is that they will have to do the teaching, play the games, and lead worship every week in addition to all the other duties involved in running the program. However, **as a sponsor, this is entirely up to you.** I have seen many frustrated sponsors who tried to do it all themselves, but that wasn't what God had called them to do. He had called them to host the program in their school, not teach it. For others, **God may be calling you to "awaken the children's or youth pastor within." In that case, DO IT!**

In most cases, our recommendation is to find a *committed* minister to do the ministry, to pastor the children. It is vital to find someone who will be committed to doing this because too many times, people say yes to everything without considering the cost. When you find that committed individual, you'll be far more effective because the children will see the same person or persons for ministry every week. Children and adults alike connect with consistency. It is a language all it's own. **Nothing says, "I care" like actually being where you are expected to be on a regular basis.** When you are there for them, they will be open and real to you. **I once heard an instructor say, "CHILDREN CAN SPOT A PHONY A MILE AWAY."** I have seen this proven over and over again. What he was referring to is the fact that children respond to consistency from their leaders and teachers. Just as animals can sense fear, children can sense sincerity. It's sad but true: Many people will want to help you for what they can gain from it. You, as a parent sponsor, play the role of a pastor; it is up to you to protect and guard those children.

When I first started Kids for Christ USA, I began by bringing in a different guest speaker every week. Please understand I am not saying don't do it this way, just that in my experience, it is not the best way. Eventually, you will run out of people you can invite to speak. Plus, you may find that the people you invite to your club have an agenda that is different from yours.

I'll never forget the impact it had on me when a parent came to me and told me that Kids for Christ was the only church their kids attended. That was the day I ceased using a different special speaker every week. It was then when I realized that there was a certain degree of "pastoring" I needed to do as the parent sponsor, and I wasn't doing it up until then. A good pastor is very careful about whom he or she allows to minister to the congregation. (That doesn't give you permission to be controlling.) Be just as wise with your Kids for Christ USA program. As you consider someone as a minister, consider this: Kids for Christ USA is designed to be a cutting-edge, "go out into the highways and hedges," kind of ministry. We believe Disney and Nickelodeon need to get their inspiration from us, not just us from them. (Don't misunderstand; I greatly respect their creativity.) By the same token, I think God has given us unlimited resources for inspiration all around us. Many people believe they are not creative, yet they walk around all day every day with ALL the creativity of the Creator of the universe living and residing in them. **So, the way I see it is that we as followers of God, AKA Christians, should be the most creative people on earth. Granted, this is just another one of my opinions, and it is not meant to belittle you; rather, it's meant to encourage you.**

Insights on Guest Speakers

Although you should probably consider having a regular speaker, guest speakers still have an important place in your Club setting. I do recommend inviting a guest speaker to come every once and a while.

It's been said that the most introverted person on the earth will influence 10,000 people in his or her lifetime. That's a staggering thought to most of us, but I believe it's also true. The first step in inviting guest speakers is drink lots of coffee (Yes, that was a joke). Next, take out a piece of paper and a pen and list the person or persons you wish to have as your weekly minister. Now pick up the phone. Don't hesitate, don't delay; call today! Get your regular minister confirmed. Then, list everyone you are able to think of as possible guest speakers. (You'll be amazed at how many you can think of.)

Please remember, how often you bring in a guest speaker is up to you. You'll get a feel for how often to do this with your group. This creates excitement, which usually increases numbers. It also gives your regular minister a break and helps him or her to be more creative.

One more point of recommendation: Ask your special speakers to arrive 30 minutes early. <u>This allows you to have time to make any last minute changes necessary in order to accommodate their needs.</u> It also gives you a cushion in case your guest gets lost or is late. When I began this ministry, my second guest speaker got lost and went to the wrong school. He arrived just at the last second before we were to start. Trust me; you don't want to experience such a scenario like I did. Just in case your guest speaker does not show up, you and / or your regular minister need to have a "back-up" service planned out. One recommendation I can give you is to make it a ritual to send them a MapQuest map with driving instructions to the school. I know this seems a bit over the top, but, after you have a guest speaker or two fail to show up because they got lost, you'll realize that this is really good advice.

I recommend that you allow ten days to two weeks at the beginning of the year to publicize your club. As we covered earlier, you have a legal right to advertise just like every other club does. And GUESS WHAT? I personally don't push this issue. I use whatever method the principal approves. In fact, none of my schools (to my knowledge) use every available means. This goes back to that martyr syndrome concept. I believe that posters and flyers are plenty effective if you're not allowed to use other means.

Promotional Schedule

In traditional school programs, there are 14 to 16 weeks per semester. We are working on a plan to work through a Kids for Christ, USA coordinator in every area across the United States. America is a big place, and this plan is therefore a work in progress. In other words, there is a very real possibility that you may find yourself preparing the schedule for the year. I advise that you diligently prepare a semester ahead. That way, you always have a "buffer," should your life become heavily committed in other areas. Life has a way of getting busy, especially for the kind of people that usually get involved in launching Bible Clubs in the schools. I believe as a mentor of mine, Rod Baker of Victory Christian Center in Tulsa said, "God's heartbeat is Souls." If you are reaching the lost of any age, you are touching God's heart and you will get busy. Plan For it!

This is a suggested promotional schedule for preparation and kick off of a club:

- Weeks 1 & 2: Use for publicity.
- Weeks 3—34: Use a Regular Minister three weeks per month and a Guest Speaker once a month.

Please understand that this is a very simple recommendation for how to promote a Club. This is one I believe in. This particular schedule allows you, the individual you choose to pastor, and the kids both variety and consistency. Maybe you truly don't know many people who qualify to be guest speakers. Obviously, you'll have to do things a little differently. It seems cliché to say it, but just relax and let the Spirit of God lead you. He really will do that.

Conducting Meetings

The recommended length of Kids for Christ USA services is 30-45 minutes, including snack time. There is no set format; this is just a suggested format. Since the Club *is your Club* as the sponsor, neither I, nor any school official, can tell you how to format your meetings. We can't tell you what to teach, or how to teach it. (Unless you wish to align your club with our organization.) For the most part, I can only make suggestions based upon my experience. I will take this opportunity to advise you of something. I believe that Bible Clubs such as KFCUSA are not the place for teaching the pet doctrines of your denomination. Including myself personally, I don't allow teaching on baptism: for or against it, dancing, musical instruments, tongues, predestination, healing, etc. I make it very clear to all ministers (guest or regular) that we teach a simple gospel message. Jesus the Christ, Him Crucified, risen again, paying for your sins, and if you believe in Him and confess it with your mouth, you will be saved. This is simple and central to all Christian denominations. We teach them a basic foundation and who the Bible says they are in Christ. We teach Biblically-based character lessons. (Which, in my viewpoint, is the only way true character can be taught.) In the next section of this book, you'll find a curriculum that we have written and recommend for the schools. You may as well use it ... you paid for it when you bought this book.

One thing to remember: in children's ministry, always be flexible. Start as close to *on time* as possible. However, keep in mind that these kids and their parents got up an hour early in order to get to school for Kids for Christ, so allow them a few minutes, if necessary, to get in and get seated.

Extended Day Programs (E.D.P.)

Many schools have Extended Day Programs (AKA on-campus daycare with a politically correct name). These are often run by the D.H.S. (Department of Human Services). Be sure you invite these kids to your meetings, as they are often the kids who need it the most. They will usually require a signed permission slip from the children's parents. (This is one reason to start the second week of school.) These programs have a schedule they normally adhere to. It would be wise to go to the person in charge of that program, introduce yourself, and simply say, "I run the Kids for Christ group. I want to be a blessing to you. We start at 8:00 A.M., and I would love to have as many of your students as possible. What can I do to help you make that happen?" In all honesty, most of them will welcome you because they have fewer children to watch during the time they're with you.

A Sample Service Schedule

8:00—8:03	High energy welcome and prayer
8:04—8:07	Fast song
8:09—8:13	Icebreaker game (Usually Boys vs. Girls)
8:14—8:17	Worship (Usually with prayer mixed in)
8:18—8:28	Message
8:29—8:30	Alter call
8:31—8:39	Snacks
8:40-	Depart to class

Just a few comments

Sometimes an upbeat (FUNNY) skit can be added in place of a game. Please notice that I said "upbeat. " I want to go on record right here (just in case someone doesn't listen): KFCUSA and Bob Heath do not endorse fear tactics to get kids saved. So, parents or school counselors, if that ever happens and you have frightened children on your hands, then remember that this ministry did not endorse that. I also don't encourage skits that make the devil out to be some big powerful guy. If you are a believer, you have all the power and life of God living in you, so you can defeat him anytime you wish. Don't portray him as being a big deal.

I always try during the worship period to ask if anyone has a prayer need. As the other kids sing, I have them all come to the front and place their hands into a "huddle" with me. Then I pray for general and/or specific needs. We must remember that we are there for them, not the other way around. Go out of your way to reach out to them, and be the face of God to these kids. Pray for them and love them. With today's high divorce rate, many of these children crave the pure love of a consistent adult in their lives. On numerous occasions, I have asked a group of children how many of their families have been through a divorce? Depending on the school and the economic level of the average kid, I have seen as many as 70% of the children raise their hands. The enemy has worked to the destroy the family; this is true, but he is also out to destroy the image of God as a Father. If he can effectively distort or destroy the image of what a father should be to his children, then he can destroy the image of God as Father. One day, as I was talking with a parent sponsor, she told me about a young boy who wanted, with all of his heart, to be a girl. She believed it had a great deal to do with the divorce of his parents. She informed me that it would be evident which boy it was. Well, as I ministered to those children that day, that boy began crying and gave his life to Jesus. (I was so blessed. I cried myself.) I just pray that the young man will be a success for his own children as a father in a few years.

Altar Calls

Since Kids for Christ is, as a friend of mine says, "a virtually untapped mission field," salvation is our highest priority. **Make your altar calls clear.** Make sure you, or those you allow to minister, don't use fear as a tactic to get children to respond. **Be very specific.** I've watched many times as guest speakers gave alter calls that leave the children unsure when to respond, so they all respond or don't respond at all because they are confused. If you have a guest, you can't always control how he or she does the altar call, but you can make what is acceptable clear to them before they start to speak. Don't discount the validity of a child's response—only God knows his or her heart, so take it at face value. A decision for Christ is a decision for Christ.

Crowd Control? In Children's Ministry

One of the most important aspects of Children's Ministry is "Crowd Control." Children will be children; which is code for "kids get rowdy." Sorry, it's just the truth. Your little angel may have a day that appears demonic. At the very least, they may begin to get a little stirred up in a crowd, especially if they're having fun. This is normal!

Since we know that children are excitable, I, as a Kid's Minister, play on it a bit. If they are excited and having fun, then you are more likely to teach them effectively. So, from my perspective, team members or parents sitting in among the children—controlling them is absolutely essential. In a perfect world, the minister is not the one that should address minor (or major) behavior issues. (He or she is "Mr." or "Miss Fun.") There should be parents or team members sitting in and around the kids to just tap them on the shoulder if they need it. Maybe even separate kids if need be. What should rarely happen is the minister needing to address the kids from the front of the room. When this happens, it makes the minister look a little impatient or double minded. On one hand, he's stirring the kids up, but on the other hand, he's telling them to calm down. Talk about mixed messages! If the whole team is functioning together, then the concept of kids ministry looking like "controlled chaos" is seen as a positive thing. What I mean is kids getting excited and the team policing them. I know that policing the crowd is something that no one likes to do. It's easier to accuse the minister of getting the kids "too excited" than to have to possibly be seen as being the bad guy/gal in the eyes of a kid.

This is one reason why I recommend having a four-person team, and as many parents involved with your Club as possible. The hidden benefit is that sitting on the floor among the kids (not along the wall) gives you a greater chance at effectively touching the lives of the children. If you sit with them consistently, they see you as a friend and they open up and share their lives with you. It's that "R" Word we all want and need improvement with: Relationship. They don't see you as the crowd police; they see you as the adult who sits with them at Kids for Christ. Sitting with them makes you become a friend, standing by the wall makes you "just another adult."

So you see, crowd control is a blessing to everyone and allows your Club to be more effective on every level.

Snacks and Prizes

When I went to the school Principal to make my petition to begin the first Kids for Christ program, the only opposition she initially raised was with regard to snacks. She was new to this school and felt as though snacks had been wrongfully used as an "enticement" at her previous school. At that school, donuts and giveaways were advertised on the posters, and she felt like that was wrong. She also didn't like donuts and would have preferred "healthy snacks." Her view of "enticements" is in a legal sense irrelevant, except that it may effect her granting you permission to have snacks for the children. My purpose in having snacks is twofold:

1. Enticement
2. Nourishment

Although the Word tells us to go out into the highways and the hedges and compel them to come in, it also tells us to "be as wise as serpents and as gentle as doves." It's a whole lot easier to get a mama to bring their child to a Bible Club that meets before school if she knows she doesn't have to feed her baby because they are going to get an acceptable breakfast supplement.

When the Principal met me with that kind of opposition, I could see I was going to need to play the game a little. I explained that due to the meeting being an hour before school started, I felt like I needed to give the children some kind of breakfast supplement. I suggested that I give them healthy snacks in lieu of breakfast. In return, I was given permission to advertise snacks one time in the school newspaper, but I was not to mention it on posters or handbills. Candy for incentives, prizes, or proper responses was not a problem. (Honestly, I probably danced a little too close to the line on this one.)

"Isn't it expensive providing snacks for 120-175 or more children every week?"

Yes, but God is faithful! You'll average at least $15-$50 a week, depending on how elaborate you go. My suggestion is to serve apples, bananas, granola bars, pop tarts, Little Debbie snacks, donuts and NO DRINKS. Drinks are too costly, too potentially messy, and too time consuming (including water). Remember, you have to get snacks in their hands and eaten, trash disposed of, and children out of the door in 10 minutes or less. Otherwise, you defeat the purpose of the snack as a breakfast supplement.

"I don't have $30-50 a week to buy snacks."

I can relate. Neither did I, but God is faithful. There are many ways to do it. Let's start with the obvious:

- As you begin your program, you may send a letter to the parents. In that letter you can tell about yourself, the program, and what your needs are in order to operate the program. Mention a need for parents to help provide some snacks.
- You can do it through corporate sponsorship.

- You can get church sponsorship or a food pantry to support you.

I have done a combination of all three ideas in my programs. The beauty of Kids for Christ is that it is very much Inter-denominational, so when it comes to the churches, they are all at least interested, and a few will get involved by donating to your program. One of the largest churches in Tulsa has a huge food pantry. They provided the majority of my snacks for several years. They also told me to let the school know that if they ever had any families in need, they wanted to help. And they did help twice, in a big way! It was awesome to be a part of that.

Funding Ideas:

We have set up KFCUSA in such a way that our funding comes on three fronts:

1. Corporate Sponsorship,
2. Church Sponsorship,
3. Individual Partners.

If you wish to have help in this area, we at KFCUSA are available to assist you. The model we have built is applicable in any area of the country. So, if you feel you would like help, our contact information is in the back of the book.

Let me give you some guidelines to start with in these three areas.

Corporate Sponsorship

Ultimately, my vision is to have a large "general fund" to back all Kids for Christ USA groups, but until that day comes, we must all raise finances for ourselves. One means of funding the program is through seeking corporate sponsorship. This is a great tool for all parties involved since they get some much desired visibility. Christian businessmen are a good source, but believe it or not, the secular businesses are often the most likely companies to get involved. With all the violence and decay in our schools, they are willing to contribute to something that might produce positive results. There is no question something needs to be done, and we have the answer.

Church Sponsorship

In all honesty, it is more difficult to acquire Church Sponsorship than Corporate Sponsorship for a variety of reasons. If a single church were to sponsor a program, they would have to be willing to be totally anonymous. Most of them just aren't willing to do that. Yet, my dream remains to have churches "sponsor" individual programs as a part of their outreach ministry. We have just launched such a program. It took years to develop, so if you'd like information, please call us.

The Supreme Court has opened the door for student-initiated Bible clubs; however, the church cannot enter the school and start an outreach program. Students and parents, on the other hand, can now begin their own Christian clubs and have any agenda the students' desire. The schools must allow students the freedom to actually start or attend their own meetings on the campus where the student attends school.

A church would simply have to silently fund the program and never interfere with the leadership of the parent sponsor. I didn't say they couldn't train the parent sponsor or offer to provide that parent with a ministry team, but for legal purposes, meetings must be multi-denominational. All qualified ministers must be welcomed, regardless of their denomination.

I have prayed for years to be a part of tearing down denominational walls. Wouldn't it be awesome if we would unite to reach the children of our city, our state and our nation for Jesus?

One idea is to get churches to sponsor us as missionaries. Who said missions needs to be overseas to be missions? Usually missionaries receive support from many different churches.

Parent sponsors often struggle with the feeling that they need to be in control. The concept of Kids for Christ USA is multiple schools all working together to reach kids in the cities, states and Nation. I've seen parent sponsors worried that a check might be sent to Kids for Christ, USA instead of to their school's program. If a check received by Kids for Christ USA is designated for your school, I'll personally see to it that you receive the funds immediately. Kids for Christ USA, Robert Heath Ministries (or Robert Heath) will not take any funds designated for a specific school.

Teacher Observers

One of the most important things to remember when attempting to minister in the schools is: Don't develop a "martyr syndrome." Everyone is not out to get you. In fact, the truth be known, there are far more caring Christian teachers who are "called of God" to minister to children as a teacher than you realize. Far too many Christians need to adjust the way they look at the rules and see them as being there to protect you. Try not to take offense and assume they are put in place to hinder you. I know that seems like common sense, but many of us have bought into the lie that the primary goal of the public school system is to further the causes of atheism. In our hearts, we know better, but we have heard the bad report for so many years that we intimidate ourselves into believing that the schools don't want us there.

Many times, schools—or school systems—require you to have a teacher present during your meetings. They are often referred to as teacher observers or teacher sponsors. **This is a good thing for you, and it's for both your protection and the school's protection.** It goes without saying that you need to have a teacher who is a believer, one with whom you will feel comfortable working.

The presence of a teacher observer can make or break your entire program.

We have worked with several schools that have no teacher observer at all. In these schools, we have truly struggled. The groups don't seem to grow. I think it gives the children and their parents the impression that the school is against the program. Rather than that, the school is taking a position of neutrality toward the program. Children identify with authority figures, and the absence of a teacher in your program can be detrimental.

It's sad. I think sometimes schools don't require a teacher observer because requiring one could make it appear that the school is supporting the program. Our society has them afraid to do what is best for everyone. I encourage you: **Don't start a club without a teacher observer.**

Good News for Teachers

When I first started KFCUSA, teacher observers were only allowed to stand by the wall and do just that: observe. However, that changed about a year and a half ago. According to Christian Educators Association International (CEAI), student clubs are split into two categories. Student-initiated clubs (that occur during the school day and after school) and clubs that simply happen to take place on the school campus. Clubs that occur during the school day in middle and high schools are governed by the Equal Access Act. That Federal statute does state that a teacher is only allowed to be at the club in a "non-participatory" capacity. (See 20 U.S.C. section 4071(c)(3).) **However, if a club occurs after school hours and just happens to be on campus, then the Equal Access Act does not apply and the restriction on teachers being involved in a "non-participatory capacity" does not apply. This is only legal if the teacher sponsors the club after school ends or while he or she is not "on the clock."** When teachers are on their own time, they may do whatever they please, just as any other private citizen would do. This means that the teacher could participate in the school club. This is truly exciting news if you are a teacher.

I know of schools where the principal was so nervous about appearing to endorse the program that he or she forbade the Club from having more than one teacher in the room. This is wrong and it's also a violation of the rights of the teachers as American citizens. The sad thing is that I know of a couple of children who happen to be the children of teachers in that school. These kids were not allowed to come to KFC meetings because of the pressure their parent (a teacher) felt from the school Principal. THIS IS WRONG!

Since we're sharing good news for teachers, here are some other exciting points:

I realize this information is not directly about Bible Clubs, but it sure is important. Have you ever had the opportunity to share your faith with a child, but you didn't think you could do it without compromising your job? Well when you—a teacher—are "off the clock," you enjoy the same rights as any other citizen. That means you can engage in witnessing activities, even if those activities happen to take place on a school campus. As a teacher you should be careful to make a distinction between your role as a teacher and your role as a private citizen. In the role as a private citizen, there is nothing to prohibit you from sharing Christ with others.

As an educator, you generally have the right to have personal items on your desk. That would also include a Bible. As long as educators do not use their position or personal items as a means of attempting to proselytize students, then personal items and even personal religious items are acceptable on a teacher's desk.

If you have more questions as a teacher concerning your rights as a Christian teacher in a public school, or if you are looking for a group of Christian teachers to affiliate yourself with, then I would strongly suggest you look into CEAI. I have had contact with this organization since we began KFCUSA. I can testify that they are top notch and they are there to make your life better. Their web site is: www.ceai.org; they are worth taking a look at.

Tools for "Doing That"

Two of the goals of Kids for Christ USA are:

- To help organize existing groups and provide resources to them.

- To see Kids for Christ groups planted in all 60,000 public schools in the USA.

Web Page

It is our ambition that Kids for Christ, USA be the ultimate source of information and inspiration for parent and student sponsors. We use primarily electronic media to communicate with our partners and friends. Please visit the site to find valuable materials to make your club a huge success.

Curriculum

For the first five years, there was really no "official" curriculum for Kids for Christ, USA. The curriculum that follows is a collaboration between myself and a close friend. The whole curriculum is a systematic walk through the Bible and is centered around the concept of equipping children to lead their friends to Jesus. In our ministry, we have witnessed the effectiveness of this concept in a way that is so extraordinary that my description would fall short. Imagine kids as young as six-years-old leading their teacher to Jesus. IT HAPPENED! Since revival is achieved one soul at a time, our primary mission in the meetings of KFCUSA is salvation. We need to reach these children for Christ and teach them to reach their friends.

I am personally not a big user of curriculum. That's because I am of the belief that I need to trust the Holy Spirit to show me what the children need in the schools I minister in. If I am sticking to curriculum, but not meeting the needs of the children, then I am not doing my job. I spend a lot of time listening, both with the ears of my spirit and the ears on my head. Please understand: I believe in curriculum or I wouldn't have taken the time to write it. I just want to encourage you to use your creativity to the fullest. Don't box yourself into our curriculum. Reach the kids!

I am developing a 35-week Virtue-based curriculum that dove-tails with the "character" program of one of the school systems in the Tulsa area. By doing this, we are reinforcing what the schools are teaching and using the truth of God's Word to do it. Look for it to be available within the year.

Kids for Christ Elementary Bible Club Curriculum
The Ticket to Heaven Prayer

The children memorize a simple salvation prayer that is split into 8 sections, (8 fingers).

The prayer is based on John 3:16, Romans 10:9,10, and John 3:3. The prayer is a weekly staple to our meetings. I have had a few random people accuse me and my organization of being "Too evangelical." I don't understand that statement, because I've read the great commission. In light of that, my viewpoint is that to be less evangelical in the schools would be more like the great omission. The only thing I can figure out is that folks who oppose children being taught to lead their friends to Jesus are trying to protect them from failure. No offense, but I can't think of a better thing to fail at. We teach children through something as meaningless as sports to learn that failure is inevitable. Yet in our spiritual lives, where we know there will be opposition... well you get the point.

It's our belief that children exposed to this program become more evangelistic, and more importantly, they become involved with their own spiritual growth. They become more aware that they can do God's work now and be very successful at it. They are quick to apply godly precepts to their personal lives because they are actually applying what they learn weekly. When children apply what they learn, they retain a much higher percentage of what is taught. When children see fruit in their own lives, it builds their relationship with God and gives them an identity in Him.

When teaching the prayer, the energy level is always high. We want them to see leading someone to Jesus as natural as eating breakfast and as fun as recess. The first couple of weeks of the school year (or whenever your club starts), try to role play with them. We start with Ticket to Heaven Practice. We have all the kids stand up, then we tell them, "When I say Thumbs up, you scream BOOOOOOM with all your might!" Of course, they are never loud enough the first time, (even if they made your ears bleed). So after they do it again, you lead them through the prayer one finger at a time.

Right Hand

1. **Thumb**—I thank you Jesus
2. **Forefinger**—You died for me
3. **Middle finger**—You rose again for me
4. **Ring finger**—Forgive all my sins
5. **Pinky**—Come into my heart

Left Hand

1. **Thumb**—Make me the champion you want me to be
2. **Forefinger**—In Jesus' name
3. **Middle finger**—Amen

After they go through it once, of course we do it again. This time in addition to the "BOOOOOM," we have them do it in a funny voice. My collaborator does "Pirate," I do "Speedy Gonzalez." I have also done "Stitch," "Scooby Doo," and any other voice they ask for that I can do. After all, the purpose is to get the prayer in their heart and head, so they can lead others to Jesus.

Now back to the *role play* I mentioned earlier. I only do this the first couple of weeks. (Only because it takes too much time.) We pair the kids off and we tell the ones on the right (Stage left) that they are giving a ticket to heaven to the person on the left. (Stage right). The one on the right asks the one on the left, "Do you have a Ticket to Heaven?" The one on the left says, "No" and naturally the one on the right asks, "Would you like one?" After the child on the left says, "Yes," then it goes back and forth using their hands walking through the prayer. In a church setting, you could go really in depth and work on overcoming objections, but in a Bible Club setting you just don't have the time.

Show and Tell: The children share their success stories of leading people to the Lord and teaching others the prayer. This is just one more way to reinforce the prayer. It's also a good way to see if the kids are getting this concept.

We have one school in the Tulsa area where two girls started doing this on their playground during their free time. It expanded as others found out about it and still others made decisions to serve Jesus with their lives. By the end of that school year, children from that school had led in the neighborhood of

450 of their peers, family and even neighbors to Jesus. The concept really works!

When an altar call is given at the end of the meeting: As children respond to the altar call, the minister brings the same number of children in front of the group. These are children who have never handed out a ticket before. Then they pray with those who responded and hand out their first ticket to heaven during the club. Helping children to overcome fear this way is so effective that often this same child hands out several more tickets during the following weeks.

Overview of Teaching Material: Monthly Themes

August

God Trusters, Doubt Busters

<u>Scripture:</u> Genesis 1:27,
"So God made man in His own image,
Male and female He created them."

September

Faith Walking

<u>Scripture:</u> 2 Corinthians 5:7,
"For we walk by faith, not by sight."

October

No Fear

<u>Scripture:</u> 2 Timothy 1:7,
"For God has not given us a spirit of fear,
but of love and power and a sound mind."

November

The Power of Thankfulness

<u>Scripture:</u> Psalm 100:9,
"Enter into His gates with thanksgiving."

December

The Birth of the Answer

<u>Scripture:</u> Luke 2:11,
"For there is born to you this day in the city
of David a Savior who is Christ the Lord."

January

The Faithfulness of God

Scripture: Hebrews 10:23,
"He who is promised is faithful."

February

God kind of Love

Scripture: 1 John 4:8,
"God is Love."

March

Releasing the power of Prayer

Scripture: Luke 11:1,
"Lord Teach us to pray."

April

The Easter story

Scripture: Philippians 3:10,
"That I may know Jesus and the
power of His resurrection."

May

Servant hood is the Mark of a Leader

Scripture: Mark 10:45,
"For even the Son of Man did not come
to be served, but to serve and to give
his life as a ransom for many."

Program Plan

- **Intro / Prayer**

  The intro must be very high energy to catch attention and the prayer must be brief and relevant.

- **Praise songs**

  The songs need to have hand and body motions to them, if possible. The group can also be separated into boys and girls. Some groups may choose to have a boys Vs. girls competition for the best "praise raisers."

- **Game**

  A great game will be remembered for weeks. Since the children you minister to are members of what I call the "Nickelodeon generation," your games must be high impact and high energy. Maybe on a "Retro" day you could do hangman, but normally the games should be more than a little crazy. In fact, "Gross and disgusting" might be a better description. Eating games and the bare feet games are some of the favorites. (Game ideas are listed in the back of this curriculum). Crazy games can be a great promotional tool. They will bring their friend for a donut, candy, and goofy games. These are also a gender war thing.

- **Confession phrase**

  The importance of having children repeat positive confessions and scriptures cannot be forgotten. Children remember what they repeat. Sports training, ABC's, music, dance, even a foreign language is taught by repetition. This teaches kids to speak life. Use the same confession all month.

- **Story** (Use the children as the characters of the story)

  All bible stories are supposed to be taught in the language of the listener. Speak kid talk when you are teaching kids. Humor, great characters and innovative object lessons all add to the memory retention of a story. Your goal as a teacher is to teach in a way that the child you teach will be able to re-teach the story to another.

- **Salvation call and training**

  After children have answered the Altar Call, bring up to the front the same number of children who have not lead someone to the Lord yet, (but they should know how to). They are brought to the front so *they* can pray with the new kids. When you do this, you are helping children bear their first fruit as they move past their own fears. At the very end of the service as the children leave, have them repeat the Ticket to Heaven Prayer.

Note: The flow of your service must start out high in energy, then slow down in the middle so that the main points of the theme are remembered, then a high energy ending to send them out the door.

Teaching Outlines

August: God Trusters, Doubt Busters

Week one (Genesis Chapter 1)

Overview: In Genesis we show the kids that God formed everything with His faith and trust in His own word. If we are then made in his image, then we are to trust Him and his word. If God is a champion and we're made in His image, then what does that make us?

Story: Genesis creation to creation of man:

Confession: God made me special, and I believe it. Who made me special?

Scripture: Genesis 1:27, "So God made man in His own image, Male and female He created them."

Ticket Practice: Introduce the Ticket to Heaven, and explain its meaning.

Week two (Genesis chapter 2 and 3)

Overview: Adam was built to believe God and His word, It was the enemy who gave us a doubt button. When he and Eve doubted God they sinned the first sin and God had to move them out of the Garden of Eden. As the manager of this world Adam handed the keys of management for the world to the enemy when he believed the enemies lie.

Story: God creating Adam and Eve to God removing them from the Garden of Eden

Confession: God made me special, and I believe it. How am I special?

Scripture: Genesis 1:27, "So God made man in His own image, Male and female He created them."

Ticket Practice: Re-introduce the Ticket to Heaven, and explain its meaning.

Week three (Genesis chapter 6:6 through Chapter 9:18)

Overview: Noah Believed God when nobody else would. God decided to start over, using Noah's family. He told Noah to build an ark, to put the animals on, along with Noah's own family. The whole time he was building, Noah tried to let people know about God's plan, but they just laughed and doubted him. Then they got on the boat, God closed and sealed the door, and the rain began. Note: Only Noah's family survived the flood. That means that no matter what color we are, we are all related. (Relate this as all mankind we are worth loving.)

Story: Noah from his command from God to the landing on Mt Arrarat.

Confession: God made me special, and I believe it. Why are you special?

Scripture: Genesis 1:27, "So God made man in His own image, Male and female He created them."

Ticket Practice: Re-introduce the Ticket to Heaven, and explain its meaning.

Week four (Genesis Chapter 12:1 through chapter 14:20)

Overview: Abram Believed God when He told him to leave his home and go to the place that God had promised. Abram believed God when He said that he would become a great nation, even though he had no children and he was pretty old to start a family. Abram and Lot separate and then he saves Lot, believing that God gave him the victory.

Story: Abram from the command of God to the saving of Lot

Confession: God made me special, and I believe it. How do I show it?

Scripture: Gen 1:27, "So God made man in His own image, Male and female He created them."

Ticket Practice: Re-introduce the Ticket to Heaven, and explain its meaning.

September: Faith Walking

Week one (Genesis Chapter 17:1 through 21:3)

Overview: Abram believed God's Word so strongly that God changed his name to Abraham. Even out in the wilderness of the "Promised Land," Abraham listened and did what God told him to do. At 100-years-old, Abraham had Isaac, his first son.

Story: Abram from his new name to the birth of Isaac.

Confession: I will act like I have a Ticket to Heaven, because God loves me just like I am. How should I act with my family?

Scripture: 2 Corinthians 5:7, "For we walk by faith, not by sight."

Ticket Practice: Let's explain why we thank Jesus in the Ticket to Heaven Prayer.

Week two (Genesis Chapter 22:1 through 22:14)

Overview: Abraham is told by God to sacrifice Isaac and Abraham believes that even if he does, God will raise Isaac up from the dead to confirm the word God gave him. (Father of many nations.) Abraham completely understood God's love for him and his son. His trust was firm.

Story: Abraham, the story of the sacrifice of Isaac.

Confession: I will act like I have a Ticket to Heaven, because God loves me just like I am. How should I act with friends?

Scripture: 2 Corinthians 5:7, "For we walk by faith, not by sight."

Ticket Practice: Let's explain why we thank Jesus in the Ticket to Heaven Prayer.

Week three (Genesis Chapter 24:1 through 24:67)

Overview: The faithfulness of Abraham's servant and how God answers prayers demonstrates that we can count on God to listen when we walk by faith.

Story: Isaac, the story of the finding of Rebecca.

Confession: I will act like I have a Ticket to Heaven, because God loves me just like I am.

Scripture: 2 Corinthians 5:7, "For we walk by faith, not by sight."

Ticket Practice: Let's explain why we thank Jesus in the Ticket to Heaven Prayer.

Week four (Genesis Chapter 27:1 through 32:30)

Overview: Jacob went from stealing his brother's blessing, to marrying Leah, to wrestling with the Lord. Although he started in fear, Jacob came to a place of relationship with God. Jacob demanded God's blessings, knowing that God always wanted him to have it.

Story: Jacob, from the stolen birthright to the wrestling with the Lord.

Confession: I will act like I have a Ticket to Heaven, because God loves me just like I am. How should I act at school?

Scripture: 2 Corinthians 5:7, "For we walk by faith, not by sight."

Ticket Practice: Let's explain why we thank Jesus in the Ticket to Heaven Prayer.

October: No Fear

Week one (Genesis 30:24 through Genesis 39:10)

Overview: Joseph was born late in life to Rachel, the wife Jacob originally arranged for with Laben. Jacob favored Joseph above his other sons. Jacob gave Joseph a coat of many colors. The coat and Joseph's dream of lording over his brothers caused great jealousy among his brothers. They sold the dreamer into slavery, but even as a slave, he kept his faith in God. He lived above the fear that could have attached itself to him and even became beloved as a slave, until he stood up to the advances of Potifer's wife.

Story: Joseph from birth to leaving Potifar's House

Confession: God is bigger than anything and anybody that's trying to make me afraid. What are you afraid of?

Scripture: 2 Timothy 1:7, "For God has not given us a spirit of fear, but of love and power and a sound mind."

Ticket Practice: Let's explain how sharing the Ticket to Heaven is nothing to be afraid of.

Week two (Genesis 39:2 through 46:31)

Overview: After overcoming the advances of Potifar's wife, Joseph found himself in jail. Joseph didn't focus on the potential failure of jail. In fact, he ended up running the jail. He interpreted the dreamd of the baker and the cup bearer, which eventually brought him before Pharaoh. From there he increased in favor to the point that he ultimately ended up second in power only to Pharaoh. After drought and famine had been in the land for years, his brothers came to Egypt for food. Joseph was the overseer of the food supply and God used him to save his family and the nation of Isreal.

Story: Joseph from prison to the saving of his family

Confession: God is bigger than anything and anybody that's trying to make me afraid. Who are you afraid of?

Scripture: 2 Timothy 1:7, "For God has not given us a spirit of fear, but of love and power and a sound mind."

Ticket Practice: Let's explain how sharing the Ticket to Heaven is nothing to be afraid of.

Week three (Exodus 1:20 through Exodus 15:4)

Overview: Pharaoh had become nervous because the Hebrews had become "many" in number. So he had ordered that baby boys be killed. Moses was born to a Levite woman. His mother and sister waterproofed a basket, placed him in it, and hid him in the reeds of the Nile. Pharoah's daughter found him and raised him as her own with the help of his own family (Unbeknownst to her). As he grew to become a man, God told him he was to be the one God would use to free his people. Through a series of events, he spent 40 years in the desert before God sent him back to Egypt to rescue His people. When God sent him, he had plenty of reasons to fear, but God had an answer for every one of them.

After Moses went to pharaoh several times, through the tool of the plagues, Pharaoh let the people go ... Then changed his mind. He chased them to the Red Sea where the Hebrews walked across on dry land and the Egyptians drowned.

Story: Moses from birth to the Red Sea.

Confession: God is bigger than anything and anybody that's trying to make me afraid. Why are you afraid?

Scripture: 2 Timothy 1:7, "For God has not given us a spirit of fear, but of love and power and a sound mind."

Ticket Practice: Let's explain how sharing the Ticket to Heaven is nothing to be afraid of.

Week four (Exodus 15:22 through Joshua 1:2)

Overview: Moses had a deep hunger and trust for God after seeing Him free his people from Egypt. This deep trust caused Moses to press into God, but the Israelites, because of fear, begged to go back to Egypt. As a result, they wandered in the wilderness for 40 years until all the original adults had passed away.

Story: Moses from Red Sea to his death.

Confession: God is bigger than anything and anybody that's trying to make me afraid. How can I defeat fear?

Scripture: 2 Timothy 1:7, "For God has not given us a spirit of fear, but of love and power and a sound mind."

Ticket Practice: Let's explain how sharing the Ticket to Heaven is nothing to be afraid of.

November: The Power of Thankfulness

Week one: (Joshua 1:1-Joshua 10:30)

Overview: Can you imagine being the understudy for years and years, then one morning you wake up and God says to you, "Moses my servant is dead ... be strong and of good courage. Joshua had the purest of responses to God: Thankfulness. After being told to gather the people, Joshua prepared for the conquest, one which included taking the fortress of Jericho. As they crossed over the Jordan, God showed He was with Joshua, just as He had be with Moses by "Piling the Jordan up in a heap" as they cross on dry land. Then when the time was right, God brought down the walls of Jericho flat with just a lot of walking, worshiping and a trumpet blast. Then the Israelites took Jericho!

Story: Joshua, From the Command from God to be strong and of good courage, to the battle of Jericho.

Confession: I will always be thankful to God for Jesus and what He did for me. Who are you thankful to?

Scripture: Psalm 100:9, "Enter into His gates with thanksgiving."

Ticket Practice: Treat or Treat report and preparation for **Operation Big Bird. Operation Big Bird** prepares the kids to offer to pray for the Thanksgiving meal. When their family says, "yes," they then ask their family to recite the Ticket to Heaven prayer and add, "and God Bless this food" at the end. In the past, our children have led thousands in the prayer and hundreds to the Lord during the Thanksgiving meal. This can be used in other holiday meal setting or in other Nations.

Week two (Judges 4:6-24)

Overview: God used Deborah to give battle plans to Barak, followed with the promise of victory. As they followed God's command, God "routed" (NIV) Sisera and all his armies and chariots by the sword.

Story: Deborah From the command of God to the Victory over Jabin the king of Canaan.

Confession: I will always be thankful to God for Jesus and what He did for me. Why are you thankful?

Scripture: Psalm 100:9, "Enter into His gates with thanksgiving."

Ticket Practice: Preparation for **Operation Big Bird.**

Week three (Judges 6:11-7:25)

Overview: Gideon goes from "shock and awe" that God would speak to him at all, let alone that He would send an angel that called him a mighty man of valor. Still in shock, he determines to test God with the fleeces, then begins to act like the man God said he was. He recruits his army only to see God whittle it down to 300 men who drink water like a dog. In fact, in Judges 7:15 it says that after the dream one of the men had was interpreted, Gideon worshiped God. Then they went out to war where they screamed and blew and God did the rest.

Story: Gideon, from the wine press to the victory over the Midianites.

Confession: I will always be thankful to God for Jesus and what He did for me. How do I show thankfulness?

Scripture: Psalm 100:9, "Enter into His gates with thanksgiving."

Ticket Practice: Preparation for **Operation Big Bird.**

Week four (Judges 16:6-30)

Overview: Delilah attempted to be a good little Philistine and trick Samson into telling her the secret of his strength. I finally spilled the beans and the Philistines tied him, gouged out his eyes and turned him into a prisoner. Samson never denied God or became unthankful to God. In fact one day while they were attempting to "make sport" of him. They stood him between the pillars of their pagan God and demanded him to perform for them. As he stood there he prayed that God grant him his strength one last time. His performance brought the house down. "Thus he killed many more when he died than while he lived".

Story: Samson, from Delilah to the falling of the Philistine temple.

Confession: I will always be thankful to God for Jesus and what He did for me. When are you thankful?

Scripture: Psalm 100:9, "Enter into His gates with thanksgiving."

Ticket Practice: Operation Big Bird.

December: Birth of the Answer

Week one (Luke 1:5-57)

Overview: Zachariah the priest and his wife Elizabeth had been unable to have children and God chose for them to be the parents of the "one who goes before," John the Baptist. When the angel came to tell Zachariah that Elizabeth would become pregnant, Zachariah did not believe the angel. God sealed his mouth. He was unable to speak until the circumcision of his son, so Zachariah wrote the name "John" for the priests.

Story: The story of the birth of John the Baptist

Confession: I believe that God loves me so much that He sent Jesus for me and for all my family. How can I make Christmas Special?

Scripture: Luke 2:11, "For there is born to you this day in the city of David a Savior who is Christ the Lord."

Ticket Practice: Putting all the names of the people that the children have prayed with onto a **birthday card to Jesus.**

Week two (Luke 2:1—24)

Overview: You know the story. You can be serious and reverent, or have a little fun with it. I personally tend to point out the parts of the story that were really miraculous: Mary minding her own business when suddenly an angel appears. In reality, you know Mary had to be a little shocked and afraid. Then the angel says the most obvious thing, "Fear not." If a Being appears in your bedroom out of thin air with the words "Fear not," would that be comforting? What if they are followed by, "you are pregnant with God's son." Mary had to be pinching herself to see if she was awake! I point out similar points with the shepherds in the field. Just make it your own. Story: The story of the Birth of Christ

Confession: I believe that God loves me so much that He sent Jesus for me and for all my family. Who can I tell the true meaning of Christmas to?

Scripture: Luke 2:11, "For there is born to you this day in the city of David a Savior who is Christ the Lord."

Ticket Practice: Putting all the names of the people that the children have prayed with onto a **birthday card to Jesus.**

Week three (Activity)

Today we put all the names of the people that the children have prayed with to receive a Ticket to Heaven onto a

birthday card to Jesus. The **birthday card to Jesus** is important because unlike the 3 wise men, these children will be giving a present to Jesus that He can keep for all eternity. The kids start seeing that **they are** a part of God's plan, not just watching it happen.

We give each child a piece of paper and two crayons. They are instructed to fold the card in half. On the front they write, "Happy Birthday Jesus." When they open the card, on the left side they write the names of all the people whom they have given a Ticket to Heaven Prayer to. On the right side they write, "These tickets to heaven are my gift to you." We then tell them to hide the card and on Christmas morning before they unwrap any gifts, give the card to Mom and Dad. "Telling them this is my gift to Jesus." It's a fun day and a tender moment in the home.

There is no fourth week in December since school is usually out for Christmas.

NOTE: Another great idea for the third week of December is the Legend of the Candy Cane. This is a story easily found on the Internet; there is also a children's book written about it. If I do this story, I usually give each child a standard size candy cane that day.

January: The Faithfulness of God

Week one (1 Samuel 1:20-1 Samuel 4)

Overview: Hannah, who had been barren, had asked the Lord to give her a son after being ridiculed at the Temple. She promised that she would give him to God and that he would serve Him all the days of his life. When he had been weaned, she took him to the temple, blessed him and left him there to serve God. She kept her promise. A prophet came and warned Eli that his wicked sons would die and their sons after them would die young. As Samuel grew in wisdom and stature, God used him to tell Eli that he too would die. Just as Samuel prophesied, it happened: the wicked sons of Eli died as the Ark of the Covenant was captured by the Philistines. Eli fell and broke his neck upon hearing the news. Samuel served God as a Prophet and a priest all his life.

Story: Samuel's story, from his birth to the death of Eli. God, Hannah and Samuel proved faithful.

Confession: I will remain faithful to God's friendship and His plan for my life.

Scripture: Hebrews 10:23, "He who is promised is faithful."

Ticket Practice: Let's explain how God is making us the Champions He wants us to be.

Week two (1 Samuel 14:1-15)

Overview: Jonathan and his dad (Saul) with a young man known only as "His Armour Bearer" had gone out to prepare for battle with the Philistines. Jonathan hatched a plan to raid the Philistines with his armor bearer. Jonathan explained a fleece that he gave God concerning whether or not they should go attack the Philistines. As it turned out, they got the "go" from God and with God's help they killed 20 men and then the philistines began killing themselves as Jonathan and his armor bearer drove the Philistines back.

Story: King Saul, Jonathan and his un-named armor bearer

Confession: I will remain faithful to God's friendship and His plan for my life.

Scripture: Hebrews 10:23, "He who is promised is faithful."

Ticket Practice: Let's explain how God is making us the Champions He wants us to be.

Week three (1 Samuel 24:6-2 Samuel 4)

Overview: David was hiding in a cave as Saul rested. David had the opportunity to kill Saul, but he didn't. He cut a piece of Saul's robe, then after he began to walk away, David called to him and exclaimed his faithfulness to Saul. A while later, Saul came with three thousand men to kill David. Again David spared him. He took Saul's spear and jug of water from beside Saul's head and called to him from the hill once again showing his loyalty. The philistines and Saul's armies went to war: Saul and his three sons were killed. After Saul's death and mourning had ended, and a long period of war between those loyal to Saul and those loyal to David, David became King of all Israel.

David fled and lived with the Philistines. In time, after nightly raids by their enemies, the Philistine King demanded that David serve with them and go to war. The other Philistines leaders refused to fight with David, so the King sent him back to camp. When they returned, they discovered that they had been raided and no one had been killed, but their wives had been taken. The men talked about stoning David. He sought God's counsel about whether he should go after the raiders. God told him to "Go," and they were successful and got the wives and other spoils of war back.

Story: God is faithful to David to make him King over Israel (from the cave to the crown).

Confession: I will remain faithful to God's friendship and His plan for my life.

Scripture: Hebrews 10:23, "He who is promised is faithful."

Ticket Practice: Let's explain how God, by His faithfulness, is making us the Champions He wants us to be.

Fourth Week (2 Samuel 11-12:4)

Overview: David stayed home while the other Kings went out to war. He was bored. One day he took a walk, and from the rooftop he saw Bathsheba bathing. She filled his thoughts, so he sent for her and slept with her. (Obviously, you clean this up with your wording as you teach the kids.) When became pregnant and sent word to David. David had Uriah (her husband) called off the battlefield to come home and relax with his wife. He wanted Uriah to think he was the father, but Uriah refused to come home. So David sent him back to the battle, but had him moved to the frontlines so that he would be killed. David did this in an effort to hide his sin. After the period of mourning was past, David married Bathsheba. God was very displeased with David for what he had done. He sent the prophet Nathan to David to confront him and David repented. The baby died, but eventually David and Bathsheba had another baby named Solomon.

Story: King David makes a mistake and God still proves His faithfulness to David and his people.

Confession: I will remain faithful to God's friendship and His plan for my life.

Scripture: Hebrews 10:23, "He who is promised is faithful."

Ticket Practice: Let's explain how God is making us the Champions He wants us to be.

February: God Kind of Love

Week one (1 Kings 3:5-15)

Overview: The Lord came to Solomon in a dream and said to him, "What do you want? Ask, and I will give it to you!" Solomon asked him for wisdom so that he might rule God's people well. God granted that request and Solomon is known even to this day as the wisest man in history.

Story: Solomon, the King loves God and His people so much that he prays for wisdom to lead them.

Confession: God's word says to love Him with all my heart, soul and mind and my neighbor as myself. How do I love God with all my heart, soul and mind?

Scripture: 1 John 4:8, "God is Love."

Ticket Practice: When we ask God into our heart, it changes how we can love and who we can love.

Week two (Matthew 22:34-40)

Overview: Jesus was questioned by the Pharisees and succeeded in silencing them. Then, one of them, who happened to be a lawyer, asked him, "What is the greatest commandment in the law?" Jesus said that loving God was, but then He said that the second commandment was equal to the first. That was loving people, and our love for other people is as important to God as our love for God himself.

Story: Jesus told the young ruler that loving people was just as important to God as our love toward God Himself is.

Confession: God's word says to love Him with all my heart, soul and mind and my neighbor as myself. When do I love people?

Scripture: 1 John 4:8, "God is Love."

Ticket Practice: When we ask God into our heart, it changes how we can love and who we can love.

Week three (Nehemiah 1-3)

Overview: When the people of Israel came back to Jerusalem from captivity, they find the city in ruins. The walls were broken down and the people were greatly disturbed by it. Nehemiah prayed, asking God to let him lead the people in rebuilding the wall. This is exactly what God did. The new wall would protect them from their enemies.

Story: Nehemiah loves God and His people so much that he prays that God would send him to lead them to build a wall of protection around Jerusalem

Confession: God's word says to love Him with all my heart, soul and mind and my neighbor as myself. Why do I love my friends?

Scripture: 1 John 4:8, "God is Love."

Ticket Practice: When we ask God into our heart, it changes how we can love and who we can love.

Week four (Esther 2:7-8:7)

Overview: Read the book; it's only eight chapters and it's an easy read. I can't summarize it better than it is written.

Story: Esther loves her people so much that she puts her life in danger when she exposes Haman's plot to kill God's children

Confession: God's word says to love Him with all my heart, soul and mind and my neighbor as myself. Why do I love my enemies or people who aren't cool … like me?

Scripture: 1 John 4:8, "God is Love."

Ticket Practice: When we ask God into our heart, it changes how we can love and who we can love.

March: Releasing the power of prayer

This is one of my favorite months. As kids learn more about how to pray, they begin to learn and experience relationship with God for themselves. Some have questioned me as to whether I really think elementary age kids get this. After six years and countless testimonies, I assure you they get it, maybe even more than we adults do. Get ready. This is a powerful month.

Week one (Matthew 6:9-13)

Overview: In my opinion, breaking down the elements of the Lord's Prayer is one of the most powerful and simplest lessons on prayer that can be taught. I break it into "Praise" (verse 9-10a), "surrender to him" (verse 10b), "provision" (v 11), "Repentance" (v 12) "Stand against sin" (v 13a), "Worship" (13b). Teach this as a way to learn how to pray. The kids really get it and your adult helpers will dig it too.

Story: Jesus teaches on prayer (the Lord's Prayer).

Confession: I will pray to my God and believe He always hears me. How do I know God hears me?

Scripture: Luke 11:1, "Lord Teach us to pray."

Ticket Practice: Practice sharing the ticket and praying for others.

Week two (Matthew 17:1-8)

Overview: Peter, James and John went with Jesus up the mountain. As Jesus prayed, His appearance changed and he "shone" like the sun. Then they saw two men with him that they said were Moses and Elijah. When Jesus returned, the men they wanted to build three shrines. Then God spoke from the cloud, "This is my beloved Son, in whom I am well pleased. Listen to Him." The Bible says the men were terrified and fell face down and worshipped God. Then Jesus came to them and touched them.

I teach the kids that this is a picture of us filled with all the fullness of God. When we pray, that light that is in us shines and we are changed. We should expect change when we pray. We should worship God, and when we do, don't be surprise if He touches our situation.

Story: Jesus prays and becomes transfigured.

Confession: I will pray to my God and believe He always hears me. Why does God hear me when I pray?

Scripture: Luke 11:1, "Lord Teach us to pray."

Ticket Practice: Practice sharing the ticket and praying for others.

Week three (John 9:1-7)

Overview: As Jesus was walking near the pool of Siloam, those with him asked about a particular man they all knew as a blind beggar. They asked him whose sins caused the man to be born blind? Jesus told them no one had sinned; he was born blind to glorify God. Jesus then prayed. Next, He spit in the dirt and made mud. Then he put the mud on the man's eyes and told him to go and wash in the pool. When he did as he was told, the blind man was suddenly able to see.

Prayer is the action that usually precedes a move from God; that is the main lesson. It doesn't matter whether it's an isolated situation that needs God's touch or a National revival; the action of prayer is needed.

Story: Jesus prays and the "blind beggar" is healed.

Confession: I will pray to my God and believe He always hears me. When does God hear me?

Scripture: Luke 11:1, "Lord Teach us to pray."

Ticket Practice: Practice sharing the ticket and praying for others.

Week four (Matthew 26:36-46)

Overview: The weight of what was before Him began to come on Jesus. As it did, He prayed these words: *"My Father! If it is possible, let this cup of suffering be taken away from me. Yet I want your will, not mine."* I usually stress to the kids the importance of turning to God and laying our troubles at His feet. I tell them that it takes great faith to say, "God, I put myself in your hands in this situation. I choose to let you handle it regardless how great the pressure."

If you don't take this as an opportunity to do an altar call or at least pray for the kids, you might be missing a precious opportunity. I encourage you, DON'T MISS IT.

Story: The prayer of Jesus in the Garden of Gethsemane.

Confession: I will pray to my God and believe He always hears me. Since I believe God hears me, what can I expect?

Scripture: Luke 11:1, "Lord Teach us to pray."

Ticket Practice: Practice sharing the ticket and praying for others.

NOTE: Don't just teach about prayer. Also teach the kids to listen for God to speak to them in their hearts.

April: Easter

Week one (Matthew 26:26-29)

Overview: In teaching this lesson, I stress the importance and power of the new covenant that the meal signifies. YES! KIDS GET IT! Don't talk down to them, but talk to them. I am not saying be heavy. Just make it your own.

Story: The Last Supper.

Confession: The power of God is in me now and forever. How do I know it?

Scripture: Philippians 3:10, "That I may know Jesus and the power of His resurrection."

Ticket Practice: Let's explain Jesus rising from the dead for each one of us.

Week two (Matthew 26:47-24:66, Mark 14:43-15:47, Luke 22:47-23:56, John 18:1-19:42)

Overview: The cross is like the rapture or the end times: If you talk to 20 people you'll hear the story 20 different ways. I have listed the story from all for gospels so you choose which one you wish to follow. Make the story "your own;" the kids connect with what you are passionate about.

Story: The Cross.

Confession: The power of God is in me now and forever. Why did God give me His power?

Scripture: Philippians 3:10, "That I may know Jesus and the power of His resurrection."

Ticket Practice: Let's explain Jesus rising from the dead for each one of us.

Week three (Matthew 28:1-15, Mark 16:1-12, Luke 24:1-49, John 20:1-30)

Overview: This time I strongly suggest you read all the above passages about the resurrection and combine them. I personally prefer to tell the story to kids from John's perspective. I especially like to poke fun at how impressed John was with his own speed. I also like to point out the image of resurrection and the concept of "New Birth" in this message. This is a fun and powerful message.

Story: The stone rolls away on the third day

Confession: The power of God is in me now and forever. What do I do with God's power?

Scripture: Philippians 3:10, "That I may know Jesus and the power of His resurrection."

Ticket Practice: Let's explain Jesus rising from the dead for each one of us.

Week four (Matthew 28:16-20, Mark 16:14-20)

Overview: The Great Commission. (This is an intro to the next month.) I point out that Jesus told the disciples about the authority He had been given and that He was giving it to us.

Story: Jesus is taken up into the sky.

Confession: The power of God is in me now and forever. When should I share His power?

Scripture: Philippians 3:10, "That I may know Jesus and the power of His resurrection."

Ticket Practice: Let's explain Jesus rising from the dead for each one of us.

May: The Great Commission

Week one (Acts 10:1-48)

Overview: Cornelius had a dream in which an angel told him to send men to Joppa for Peter. He sent them as he was instructed. While they were coming, Peter had the vision of the sheet full of "unclean" animals. In it, he was told three times, "Rise Peter, kill and eat." Peter's response the first two times was, "I have never eaten anything unclean." The third time God told him not to call unclean what He called clean. At that moment, the vision ended and Peter looked up just as Cornelius' men arrived. Peter went with them and the household of Cornelius was saved.

Story: Peter visits Cornelius.

Confession: All of creation is waiting for the Jesus in me to come to them. What do I do to show Him to them?

Scripture: Mark 16:15, "Go into all the world and preach the Gospel to every creature."

Ticket Practice: Practice the ticket in an alternate language.

Week two (Acts 12:25-14:28)

Overview: After Paul's commissioning by the apostles, they went out on their first Missionary trip together. They cast out demons in Cyprus, preached revival services in Antioch and Pisidia, and saw great signs and wonders in Iconium. They were stoned in Lystra, and cared for the people they had previously ministered to in Antioch as they headed Home.

Story: Paul and Barnabas go on their first journey.

Confession: All of creation is waiting for the Jesus in me to come to them. How do I show Jesus to others

Scripture: Mark 16:15, "Go into all the world and preach the Gospel to every creature."

Ticket Practice: Practice the ticket in an alternate language

Week three (Acts 18:23-21-14)

Overview: The trip began with a bang with ministry, miracles, and ultimately rioting in Ephesus. Paul then journeyed into Greece, preached all night at Troas, then after his farewell address to the Ephesian elders, he headed out to Miletus. At the end of the journey he had a prophetic warning by Agabus about him being bound in Jerusalem.

Story: Paul goes on his second journey.

Confession: All of creation is waiting for the Jesus in me to come to them. When can I share the Jesus in me with them?

Scripture: Mark 16:15, "Go into all the world and preach the Gospel to every creature."

Ticket Practice: Practice the ticket in an alternate language

Week four (21:15-28:31)

Overview: Shortly after his return to Jerusalem, Paul was arrested (as prophesied by Agabus). After getting no where in his defense, He appealed to Caesar and the rest of the book deals with that journey.

NOTE: Most schools will be out for the summer before you teach this lesson. We included it just "in case."

Story: Paul goes to Rome.

Confession: All of creation is waiting for the Jesus in me to come to them. Where can I share the Jesus in me with them?

Scripture: Mark 16:15, "Go into all the world and preach the Gospel to every creature."

Ticket Practice: Practice the ticket in an alternate language.

Games

NOTE: Neither I, Robert Heath, nor Kids for Christ, USA endorse or recommend the game "Chubby Bunny" in any form! Just in case you are not aware of what I mean by Chubby Bunny, it is a game in which its participants stuff as many marshmallows as possible into their mouths while repeating the words Chubby Bunny. In fact, we advise against any games involving eating of marshmallows, peanut butter, spam or any fish products. It's too easy for "bad things" to happen.

Next, for the sake of not being redundant, I did not write the following in the description of every game listed below under materials needed: Most games require a trash can and are a lot more fun with some type of high energy background music.

And now, On with the Games:

Old Yeller

Borrowed by Bob Heath from a forgotten source. (I can't even remember its origin. I've used it so long it seems like my own.)

As many contestants as you wish.

Materials Needed: 1 Alka Seltzer tablet and cup of water per contestant, Large lined trash can.

How to Play: Give each person an Alka Seltzer tablet and begin to explain to them the object of the game. They are to place the tablet into their mouth. Explain to them and the crowd that the tablet is going to begin to foam. Tell them, "Do not swallow the foam." After a few seconds you give them each a sip of water. Remind them not to swallow. Tell them when they can't stand it any more, spit the tablet and foam into the trash can. With any luck the foam will begin to ooze out of their mouths and they'll look like "Old Yeller." The object of the game is to be the last one standing with the tablet and foam still in their mouth.

Cheese Balls and Toe Jam

Created by Bob Heath

2-4 Contestants

Materials needed: Cheetos Cheeseballs, Paper Plates.

How to Play: Place 10 cheeseballs on each plate. Place the plate on the floor in front of the contestants. Then instruct them to remove their right shoe and sock. The object of the game is to be the first one to eat all their cheeseballs with their toes. No hands allowed. (Except to assist the foot in getting to the mouth.)

Open Bible Relay

Created by Shelly Heath

Unlimited Contestants

2 Bibles

How to play: This is a relay and is designed for a gym. Divide into two teams, then set up your relay. Open both Bibles to the same place. Hand the Bible to two people at the beginning of the line. The idea is that the kids run back and forth and the pages turn as they run. The team whose Bible is the closest to the original start point wins.

Frozen Donuts

Created by Lizzy Strauss

<u>Unlimited Contestants</u>

<u>Materials Needed:</u> One frozen donut for each contestant.

<u>How to Play:</u> This one is pretty obvious. Contestants compete in attempting to be the first to eat a frozen donut.

Blindfolded Banana eating contest: A funny/cruel joke

Created by a former KFCUSA team member

<u>2-4 Contestants:</u> Works best Boys Vs. Girls

<u>One banana per contestant</u>

<u>How to play:</u> Send the contestants into the hallway. When they get outside you tell the audience to keep cheering and don't let the players in on the secret. Blindfold each contestant, then hand each of them a banana. As you begin to count down the start, you remove the blindfold(s) from the girls. On three you yell go and watch the boys attempt to find their mouth. When they are almost done you yell GIRLS WIN and remove the boys blindfolds and let them in on the joke.

Feet of Feet

Created by Bob Heath

2-4 Contestants

Materials Needed: 2-4 Fruit Rollups.

How to Play: After giving each contestant a wrapped fruit rollup, instruct them that they may un-wrap the fruit rollup with their hands, and eat it. However they must take off their shoes and separate the plastic and the fruit rollup with their toes. Then they must eat the fruit rollup with their feet too. First one finished wins.

Bird Seed Eating Contest

Created by Bob Heath

2-4 Contestants

Materials Needed: Shelled sunflower seeds, 2-4 pie pans.

How to play: After choosing you contestants, tell them to get on their knees and place their hands behind their backs. Cover the bottom of the pie pan with seeds. Then instruct the contestants to eat the seeds like a bird. Be sure you get the kids to smile at the crowd when your done. IT"S A SCREAM! (And a great photo op.)

Whipped Cream Fountain

Created by Bob Heath

2-4 Contestants

Materials Needed: 2-4 Balloons, one large can of Whipped Cream

How to play: As you chose your contestants, it is imperative that they are advised of the "no chicken out rule." This one isn't gross, but it can be messy. When you have your contestants standing there, hand each of them a balloon. Then grab the whipped cream (which has been hidden until now). Take a balloon, place the stem of the whipped cream can in the balloon and proceed to fill the balloon. Hint: One thing I didn't count on when I did this game was the fact that the aerosol in the can will inflate the balloon, so for safety sake, you will need to let most of the air out of the balloon before you hand it to the children. NOW you're ready to play: Tell them that the first person/team to suck the whipped cream out of the balloon wins.

Whipped Cream Slurp

Created by Bob Heath

2-4 Contestants

Materials Needed: 2 cans of whipped cream, 2-4 throw away pie pans, 2-4 straws.

How to Play: After selecting your contestants, place a pie pan on the floor in front of each contestant. Then direct each contestant to get on their knees and hand each one a straw. Explain to them that they have to suck all the whipped cream from their pie pan with a straw. This is tougher than it sounds; you'll usually have to "judge" who actually won.

Whipped Cream Slurp (Variation 2)

Created by Bob Heath

2-4 Contestants

Materials Needed: 2 cans of whipped cream, 2-4 throw away pie pans, plenty of paper towels.

How to Play: After selecting your contestants, place a pie pan on the floor in front of each contestant. Then direct each contestant to get on their knees and place their hand behind their back. They will slurp as much whipped cream as possible "with their face." Clearly this version can be a bit messy.

Jell-O Slurping

Oldest game in Children's ministry

2-4 Contestants

Materials needed: 2-4 Jell-O cups, 2-4 straws,

How to Play: After selecting your contestants, hand each one a cup of Jell-O and a straw. Peel the lid of the Jell-O back just a smidge and place your straw in the Jell-O. On the count of three, they begin slurping the Jell-O until someone finishes.

Jell-O Eating (Variation 1)

Created by Bob Heath

<u>2-4 Contestants</u>

<u>Materials needed:</u> 2-4 Jell-O cups (liquefied), 2-4 knee high hose, 2-4 trash bags w/three holes for arms and head.

<u>How to Play:</u> After selecting your contestants, place a trash bag over their upper body to protect their clothes. Then hand each one a cup of liquefied Jell-O and a knee high. Instruct them to pull the knee high over their head down to their mouths (no further) Peel the lid of the Jell-O back just a smidge and tell them that on the count of three they need to be the first one to drink all the Jell-O through the knee high.

Jell-O Eating (Variation 2)

Created by Bob Heath

<u>2 Contestants</u>

<u>Materials needed:</u> 2 bowls of cubed Jell-O, 2-4 toothpicks, 2 empty bowls

<u>How to Play:</u> Each contestant will take a toothpick in their teeth, kneel (can be done on a table) and put their hands behind their back. The object is obvious; move all the Jell-O cubes from one bowl to the other only using the toothpick in their mouth.

Bobbing for Ravioli

Created by Matthew Wofford (Former team member, 2002)

2 Contestants

Material needed: 4 medium sized bowls, 4 cans Spaghetti O's, 2 cans ravioli, two plastic bags, two plastic bags with holes cut for head and arms, plenty of paper towels.

How to Play: Before your meeting: Empty the raviolis into the bottom of two of the bowls. Cover the ravioli with spaghetti O's. Next, after you select your contestants, place a clothes protector (AKA: plastic bag) over your contestants. Then two bags on the floor to protect it. Place the full bowls on the bag with an empty bowl next to it. The rest is self explanatory; the contestants bob for ravioli through the Spaghetti O's.

Dirty Diaper Eating Contest

Created by Matthew Wofford (Former team member, 2002)

2 Contestants:

Materials needed: 2 disposable diapers, peanut butter, 4 Oreo cookies and a spoon.

How to Play: Before you begin, smear a spoonful of peanut butter on each diaper. Then crumble two Oreo's up and place them in each diaper. Mix the two together well and use the spoon to smear them into the bottom enough that it looks like an actual dirty diaper. First, as you select your contestants BE SURE THAT YOUR CONTESTANTS ARE NOT ALERGIC TO PEANUT BUTTER.

Explain to your contestants and the crowd that they will be eating the contents of the diaper. Be sure also to let everyone know that they are really not eating from a dirty diaper. One, two, three: GO!

Baby Food Slurp

Created by Bob Heath

<u>2-4 Contestants</u>

<u>Materials needed:</u> 2-4 jars of banana baby food, 2-4 straws.

<u>How to Play:</u> Each contestant is to slurp the contents of a jar of baby food with a straw.

Fun with Pickles

Because of the fact that 50% of children think pickles to be "gross," games with pickles are a scream! Hear are a few:

Pickles Eating Contest

Honestly is there really a creator?

<u>2-4 Contestants</u>

<u>Materials needed:</u> 2-4 Pickles.

<u>How to Play:</u> After you pump up the crowd, hand each of your contestants a pickle. On your mark get set GO!

The Pickle Dog

Created by Bob Heath

2-4 Contestants

Materials needed: 2-4 Hot dog buns, 2-4 pickles, 1 can of whipped cream, fork.

How to Play: After you select your contestants, hand each of them a hot dog bun with a pickle in it. (I said PICKLE, not pickle spear.) Then top each one with whipped cream. Have fun!!

Making Pickle Juice

Created by Dr. Gary R Lee

2-4 Contestants

Materials Needed: 2-4 Pickles, 2-4 clear plastic cups.

How to Play: Select your contestants, then hand each of them a Pickle and a cup. The object is to "juice" the pickle with their mouths. (It can be a bit chunky.) The one who produces the most juice wins.

Pickle Juice Drinking Contest

Created by Bob Heath

2 Contestants:

Materials Needed: A jar of pickle juice, 2 cups.

How to Play: Divide your pickle juice into to two cups, then at the three count the first one finished wins.

Pickle Juice Drinking Contest (Variation 2)

Created by Bob Heath

2 Contestants:

Materials Needed: A jar of pickle juice, 2 baby bottles.

How to Play: Divide your pickle juice into to two baby bottles, then at the three count the first one finished wins.

Jelly Filled Pickle

Created by Bob Heath

2 Contestants

Materials Needed: A pumpkin carving tool, 2 pickles, a squeeze jar of jelly.

How To Play: The preparation on this one is a labor of love. Using your pumpkin carving tool, core a pickle end to end. (At least half way.) After you select your contestants, squeeze the jelly into the pickle. First one to eat the pickle wins.

Pudding Face

Created by Jon Gentry (KFCUSA Team Member 2006-2007)

4 Contestants: Two Feeders and Two servers.

Materials Needed: 2 thin four foot dowel rods, 2 pudding cups, and 2 plastic spoons.

How to Play: First, before you begin your meeting, tape a spoon to the end of each of your dowel rods. (I don't advise pre-opening your pudding, it could be a significant distraction.) Select two boys and two girls as your contestants. (It's really funny with a short/younger child feeding a taller/older child.) Once you have your contestants, open the pudding and hand it to the child who will be fed. Hand the dowel rod to the younger/shorter contestant. On the count of three begin. Obviously, the first team done wins.

Silly String Glasses

Created by Reagan Saunders (KFCUSA Team Member 2006-2007)

4 Contestants: Two Boys, Two Girls.

Materials Needed: 2 Trash Bags, 2 pair of large goofy sunglasses, 2 cans silly string.

How to Play: Cut arm and head holes in each of the trash bags. Assist one member of each team in putting on the trash bag. Then hand the glasses to the same two kids. Explain to the other two kids and the crowd that they are to shoot as much Silly String as possible on the glasses of the other person from six feet away. IT'S FUNNY!

Acting Class

Created by Bob Heath

4-6 Contestants: Any more than six takes way too long.

NO MATERIALS NEEDED

How to play: This game can be used as often as you like with a different acting assignment. My personal favorite is as follows: After picking your contestants, inform the crowd that they will be the judges of an acting contest. "This is not a popularity contest" is a very important part of the instructions to the judges. Then you inform the contestants that they are going to be doing a little "acting." One at a time, give each contestant 15-30 seconds to act like popcorn popping. It is a scream!When they have all had their turn, then the crowd judges by applause.

Acting Class Part 2

I can't remember the source.

How to play: Another variation that I have seen done, and don't know its origin is: Send your actors out in the hall with a leader. Close the door. (Closing the door is very important.) Once they are outside, the leader who is inside explains the role of the crowd as judges and tells them that each kid is going to be acting out the first time they used the potty by themselves. Out in the hall, you tell the contestants that they are to act out the first time they rode a rollercoaster. IT IS HYSTERICAL! After the judging, you tell the contestants and the judges what you did.

Frozen Waffle Tossing

Created by Bob Heath

4 Contestants: Two on each team.

Materials Needed: Two boxes of frozen waffles. (Whipped cream if you'd like.) Two paper plates.

How To Play: Select one contestant on each team to lie down on their back. Have them lay parallel to each other. Then hand them a paper plate, which they will hold above their chest, but below their chin. Have the other two contestants stand 6-10 feet away from the feet of the one lying down. (The distance varies based on the age of the contestants.) Then hand them an open box of frozen waffles. Instruct them that all they have to do is toss the waffles onto their team mates plate. The team with the most waffles parked on the plate wins. If you wish a little shock factor, add a squirt of whipped cream on each waffle before it's tossed. (If you choose this option, you might want to cut arm and head holes in a trash bag and place it over the contestants lying down.

CoCo Puff Relay

I'm not sure who created it.

10-40 contestants

Materials Needed: 2 CoCo Puffs

How to Play: Determine how many you want to include in this game. Divide the number into four groups. Separate two lines, 20 feet apart for each team. Instruct the group that this is a relay and that they need to be on their hands and knees. Place a coco puff in front of the lead person on both teams. On three they are to push the coco puff to the other end with their nose.

CoCo Puff Relay (Variation 2)

Created by Bob Heath

<u>10-40 contestants</u>

<u>Materials Needed:</u> 2 CoCo Puffs, 10-40 straws.

<u>How to Play:</u> Determine how many you want to include in this game. Divide the number into four groups. Separate two lines, 20 feet apart for each team. Instruct the group that this is a relay and that they need to be on their hands and knees. Place a coco puff in front of the lead person on both teams. On three they are to push the coco puff to the other end with their straw.

Making Sandwiches

Created by Former KFCUSA Team Members

<u>2-4 Contestants</u>

<u>Materials Needed:</u> 2-4 paper plates, 4-8 slices of bread, 2-4 spoonfuls of Peanut Butter, 2-4 spoonfuls of Jelly.

<u>How to Play:</u> Be certain as you select your contestants that you stress that NO ONE SHOULD VOLUNTEER IF THEY ARE ALLERGIC TO PEANUT BUTTER. After you pick your contestants, you place 2 pieces of bread, one spoonful of peanut butter, and one spoonful of jelly on each plate. (It's good to have an assistant help with this game or the set up takes way too long.) You then explain to the contestants that they are to make a PB&J sandwich WITH THEIR TOUNGES! They can only use their hands to hold the plate.

Gargle a Tune

The source unknown.

2-4 Contestants

Materials: 2-4 Cans of 7-up or Sprite (Something clear).

How to Play: Give each contestant a can of pop. I like the ABC song as the tune the contestants need to gargle. This is a timed event and can be funny!

Ice Cream Surprise

Created by Bob Heath and a former team member

2-4 Contestants

Materials: 2-4 sugar cones, 1 can sweet peas, 1 can of whipped cream.

How to Play: Drain the can of peas before the meeting begins. Then place a spoonful or two of peas in each cone. Keep you cones well hidden until you are about to hand them to your contestants. I play this up as a whipped cream cone eating contest with a surprise inside. Before you hand each contestant their cone, squirt whipped cream on top of the cone. One the count of three, your contestants will inhale their cone. The looks are priceless when they hit the peas.

Hula Hoop Relay

Creator unknown.

5-10 Contestants

Materials Needed: 2 Hula Hoops.

How to Play: Start with the person at the front of the line. Each time the hula hoop hits, the next person in line begins to hula. The first team through the line loses.

Hula Hoop Transfer

Creator unknown

20 or more Contestants

Materials Needed: 2 Hula Hoops.

How to Play: Divide into two teams, then grab hands and stretch the line. Give the Hula Hoop to the person at the beginning of each team's line. Explain that the object is to transfer the hula hoop to the other end of the line without letting go of each other's hand.

Traditional Hula Hoop Contestant

Creator unknown

2 contestants

Materials needed: 2 Hula Hoops.

How to play: Do I really need to explain? (I didn't think so.) One point: Put a time limit on this one.

Template for School Newspaper Ad

Kids for Christ is Coming to [insert your school name]!

Join us beginning **[insert the weekday, month, day, and year]** @ **[insert the start and stop times].** We will meet in the **[insert the location].** The mission of this organization is to let students know they have other Christian friends at school. Each week healthy snacks will be purchased for every child who would like one. Meetings will consist of games, songs, object lessons and a short message. The meetings are high energy and **lots of fun!**

Kids for Christ Parent Info Letter

VERY IMPORTANT NOTE: <u>The below letter is included as an example, NOT a TEMPLATE.</u> *Here's why: You as a parent sponsor could write a letter like this about yourself. I think that's a good idea. You must, however, be careful if you tell your school about me or about Kids for Christ, USA. Why? It may give the impression that an outside ministry is invading the school and that the school is supporting it. So when you publicize about your club, make it fun! Keep it local. And keep it simple: Who, What, When, Where, Why. We'll all stay out of trouble that way.*

Incidentally, if you contact us, we have a generic flyer that you can customize with the appropriate information for your school.

Dear Parents,

My Name is Robert (Bob) Heath and I am writing this to inform you of a new program before school at 8:00-8:40 every Wednesday, beginning January 10, 2001 in the Media Center.

I have served as a Children's Pastor, Youth Minister, and also have done what I called "Festival Ministry" in Jenks. Shelly and I have been married for 15 years and have three sons (two of which attend McAuliffe). I expect our Kids for Christ at McAuliffe to be exciting! The kids will love it! I pray you'll allow your children to attend. I have invited several different area ministers, athletes, and musicians to come and share with the kids this year. If you know someone who might be willing to come, please let me know.

The mission of this organization is to let students know that they have other Christian friends at school and provide an awesome tool for ministering to friends who have not had the opportunity to know Jesus.

The memory verse for this year is II Timothy 1:7, "God has not given us a spirit of fear but of power, love, and a sound mind."

The service consists of games, songs, and object lessons. All services are high energy and lots of FUN!

Each week healthy snacks are purchased for every child who would like one. We have other prizes for games.

As you are probably aware, programs like this cost money. If you would like to help support this outreach, it would be greatly appreciated. You can assist us by donating: cash, fruit and granola bars, or candy for prizes. If you donate cash, understand it will be used to purchase snacks or prizes. If you have any questions, please contact Robert Heath at 459-8808 (home) or 902-2442 (mobile).

Please pray, as this year is McAuliffe's first ever Kids for Christ program. I am praying that this program will be a huge success and just the foundation for an even more successful year next year!

Thanks,

Robert C. Heath

A Cute Idea

The following is a letter my son, Boston, gave to all his kindergarten friends:

I have a lot of fun at Kids for Christ. We meet before school on Wednesday mornings from 8:00-8:40. Cool people come and talk to us. We play games, and sing fun songs, and we even have a snack at the end.

I'd like to invite my whole class to come.

Your Friend,

Boston Heath

Generic Permission Slip

Kids for Christ Permission Slip

Name of Child: _____

Child's Address: _____

_____

_____

Email address: _____

Home Phone:_____ Cell Phone: _____

Name of Parent or Guardian: _____

Signature of Parent or Guardian: _____

By signing this, you are giving your child permission to attend and participate in the Kids For Christ Bible Club. If you add your email address we can keep you updated better as to what we are doing.
